EASTER ISLAND

Island of Enigmas

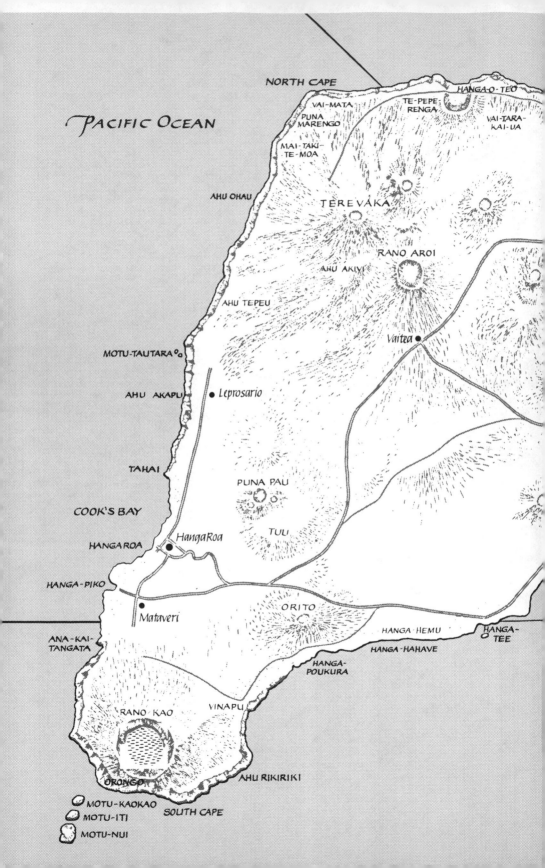

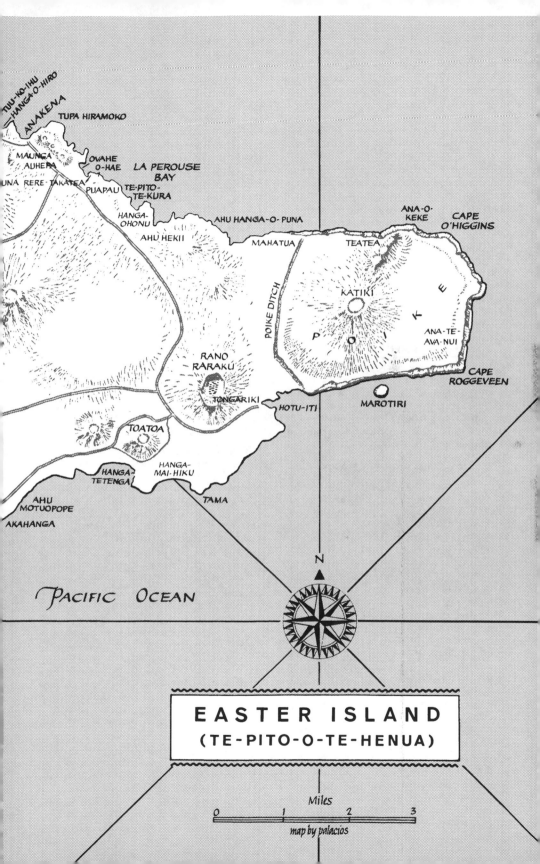

TUU-KO-IHU
HANGA-O-HIRO
ANAKENA
TUPA HIRAMOKO

MAUNGA
AUHEPA
OVAHE
O-HAE
LA PEROUSE
BAY
UNA RERE-TAKATEA
PUAPAU
TE-PITO-
TE-KURA

HANGA-
OHONU
AHU HANGA-O-PUNA
AHU HEKII
MAHATUA
TEATEA
ANA-O-
KEKE
CAPE
O'HIGGINS

POIKE DITCH
KATIKI
E
K
I
P O

RANO
RARAKÚ
O

ANA-TE-
AVA-NUI

CAPE
ROGGEVEEN

TONGARIKI
HOTU-ITI
MAROTIRI

TOATOA

HANGA-
MAI-HIKU

HANGA-
TETENGA
TAMA

AHU
MOTUOPOPE
AKAHANGA

PACIFIC OCEAN

N

EASTER ISLAND
(TE-PITO-O-TE-HENUA)

Miles

0   1   2   3

map by palacios

Easter Island

Island of Enigmas

JOHN DOS PASSOS

PUBLISHED BY DOUBLEDAY
a division of Random House, Inc.

Acknowledgment is made to Editions Calmann-Lévy for permission to use
a translation by John Dos Passos of "Une Viste à I'lle de Pâques"
from *Reflets sous la sombre route* by Pierre Loti, Co. 1899

DOUBLEDAY and the portrayal of an anchor with
a dolphin are registered trademarks of Doubleday,
a division of Random House, Inc.

Original Jacket Photo by George Holton
Original Jacket Typography by Rallou Malliarakis

The Library of Congress has cataloged the
hardcover edition as:
LIbrary of Congress Catalog Card Number 78-111160

A hardcover edition of this book was published in 1971 by Doubleday

First shortrun edition published 2004
Shortrun Edition: 978-0-385-51361-6

145052501

CONTENTS

LIST OF ILLUSTRATIONS

EASTER ISLAND

Island of Enigmas

I

INTRODUCTION TO EASTER ISLAND

A Rough Darkgray Statue

"Why Easter Island?" people ask.

The explanation is simple.

When I was a small boy forlornly attending an English preparatory school in the early years of this century, some kind person took me to the British Museum. There I saw a statue. This was a huge rough darkgray statue with a long sad darkgray face. As I remember it stood under some sort of arcade. I stopped in my tracks and stared at it through the sooty London drizzle. The statue stared back out of deepsunken eyes. What was it trying to say? To this day I can remember the feeling it gave me of savage brooding melancholy. When, some time later, I looked up the word enigma in a dictionary, a sort of afterimage of the Easter Island statue swam between me and the printed page. I was a great reader of Captain Cook's *Voyages*. His accounts of the island's ruined civilization finished the job. It was inevitable that, when a convenient opportunity arose, I should pick up and go.

When I began reading up for the trip I found myself in an archaeological hornets' nest. That enterprising Norwegian Thor Heyerdahl had all the authorities by the ears. He claimed that the bearers of the high stoneage culture which produced the weird civilization of Easter Island had sailed west, during some period long before the Incas, on seagoing rafts from the coast of Peru. He went on to prove that such navigation was possible by safely crossing an immense expanse of open ocean on the seagoing raft *Kon-Tiki*, which ended up on a reef in the Low Archipelago a good thousand miles farther west than Easter Island. He capped that experiment by conducting a few years later about the most thorough archaeological rummaging of Rapa Nui, as Easter Island is now known, that anyone had ever accomplished. He assembled his conclusions in a copious series of reports. In *American Indians of the Pacific* he launched the theory that the later Polynesian immigrants were part of a wave of Polynesian navigators who entered the Pacific island world from the north through Hawaii.

The older authorities meanwhile insisted that this was rubbish. The Polynesian immigration had come from the west through Malaysia. Either theory had trouble accounting for the unique features of the Easter Island culture. The archaeologists' and ethnographers' story was that it had grown up spontaneously in this isolated outpost of the Polynesian peoples.

To a layman thumbing through the arguments it seemed that nobody had assembled quite enough data to prove his point, but that each side had managed to undermine its opponents' hypothesis.

Enigma piled on enigma. Reason enough for a trip for anyone who has an ounce of curiosity in his veins.

Father Sebastian

The first living Easter Islander we met was Father Sebastian Englert. He had qualified for citizenship by thirty-three years as the island's chief missionary and father-confessor. His name through the years had become almost synonymous with the Easter Island culture. We were luckier than we knew to find him in New York, in November of 1968.

It was a horribly cold northwest day in New York. We were waiting for him in a little French restaurant on Fifty-third Street in one of those rows of multilingual restaurants that could be found almost anywhere in the world. He came in shivering. All he had to keep him warm was a brown Capuchin habit; someone had thrown a black ecclesiastical overcoat over it.

We immediately ordered some hot soup. He held his hands over the steam like a child. While he was spooning it in he thawed out. It turns out that he's a Bavarian. While spooning in the soup he brought out in thoroughly Teutonic form a curriculum vitae, which he had written out for Mrs. Hotchner, who was escorting him around New York. Born November 17, 1888, in Dillingen an der Donau, schooling the Eidstadt elementary school. Then nine years at the Gymnasium at Berghausen before he could be ordained a priest. His father was rector of the Gymnasium in Berghausen. After producing thirteen children the elder Englert was qualified for the priesthood by a special papal dispensation. The elder Englert taught Latin, Greek, French and history.

Sebastian's mother died in 1922 and a few days later, having been ordained a priest, Sebastian left for Chile to accept a post as missionary to the Araucanian Indians.

From the first he treated the aborigines as equals. He showed tremendous respect for the natives of Easter Island because, so he told us, they valued modesty more than any other quality. One of the reasons they accepted him so wholeheartedly was that in spite of the medals and awards he received from European learned societies there was no change in his attitude toward the people.

He carried the Franciscan spirit so far that for one period he tried to live with the lepers in the leper colony, but his superiors in his church on the mainland told him he was doing more good outside.

We tried to get him to eat something more solid than soup but he claimed that he had had enough. He was obviously enjoying New York in spite of the cold. He glanced around with interest at the other people in the restaurant. While he finished his soup in little spoonfuls like a schoolboy on his good behavior we thought up topics connected with Easter Island. He was no lecturer—he answered questions freely and simply. There was so much, he kept saying, he didn't know. He had come to New York and Washington to help with an exhibition of Easter Island art being prepared at the Pan American Union.

After lunch we took him in a cab to the Museum of Natural History. Mrs. Hotchner, a very able lady then doing publicity

for Lindblad Travel, had paved the way for us with some tele-
phone calls. We walked through the hall of habitat groups. Father
Sebastian was looking from side to side with sharp curiosity. At
eighty he was still mentally indexing everything he saw.

Mrs. Hotchner had arranged for us to see a famous anthropologist who took the first samples of blood types on the island.
He turned out to be very much the established scholar. He detailed a young assistant to show us the Easter Island things. These
were mostly articles of unknown origin donated by various col-
lectors. Father Sebastian was particularly pleased with a ceremonial
stone fishhook from an early period. We saw another later in his
collection on the island at Hangaroa village. We stepped aside
to let the famous anthropologist talk privately with Father Sebastian.

When we went back into the room they were arguing about
Heyerdahl. "But what's the use of a new theory?" the famous
anthropologist was saying. "The old one is firmly established. The
Polynesians moved east from the coast of China through Malaya,
stopping off in the Melanesian islands on the way."

Father Sebastian was smiling through his little beard and shaking
his head gently from side to side. The anthropologist seemed to
have no further wish to ask him questions or to prolong the interview. He did not seem to realize that he was talking to the man
who, since Sir Percy Buck's death, knew most about Pacific an-
thropology by direct experience. He seemed to have very little
curiosity about any of the Easter Island problems. As a young
man he had made the studies of blood samples which found Type
B blood almost lacking on the island. Competent experts agreed
with him, and that was that. We came away disappointed.

Mrs. Hotchner went home. My wife and I took Father Sebastian in a cab to his monastery, part of St. John's Church, across
from what was then the Pennsylvania Station. His steps faltered a
little as he went across the pavement. The wind blew in icy gusts.
It was with relief that we saw the tiny figure disappear into the
shelter of the dimly lit hall.

Father Sebastian died in New Orleans in early January, of
cancer, we were told when we arrived in Santiago de Chile later

4

that month. It was a great disappointment. We had hoped to pester him with many questions during our stay on the island.

The Pascuenses

We had read so much of the degeneracy and mongrel blood of the Easter Islanders that it was a surprise to find the group gathered for goodbyes at the Cerrillos Airport in Santiago, from which the Pacific planes took off, distinctive in manners and appearance. Especially the men had the elongated bony structure in their faces we decided later produced the special "Easter Island look." There was a quiet charm about them. There seemed to be a family relationship. Obviously none of them were rich but they were all decently dressed.

They crowded around the passengers with packages, explaining in low voices that sending them by hand was the only way they could get packages to their relatives. Air freight rates were prohibitive.

The bundles were all neatly tied up. We noticed a number of them weighed down with hams. For a while the steward asked us not to accept any bundles until he knew what the weights were going to be on the plane. The package my wife and I finally carried, for a Mrs. Beri Beri, had a dozen smaller packages inside, neatly wrapped in pink and green papers and all carefully labeled for various recipients on the island.

That night everyone was put out by the sudden announcement at about 3 A.M. that the flight had been postponed for twenty-four hours. Back to bed in the hotel. The next night the same cast of characters appeared as tactful as ever in the dingy dark. On that occasion the plane took off on time. We barely had time to notice how much more comfortable for the passengers the old prop plane was than modern jets before we fell asleep.

II

ROGGEVEEN'S MISFORTUNE

Jacob Roggeveen's little flotilla, consisting of three small ships, was sent out by the directors of the Dutch West India Company in 1721. The Dutch West India Company had never been as successful as the East India Company, which had raked in millions of guilders by despoiling the Portuguese of their trading posts in the East Indies and Japan and had furthermore sponsored Tasman's extraordinary discoveries around the Australian coasts. During the seventeenth century the West India Company had to its credit the occupation of Pernambuco and Portuguese slavetrading posts along the African coast, and the establishment of the Dutch colonies in the Hudson Valley. In the early seventeen hundreds the company was reorganized. An English publication on the South Seas gave the new directors the hope that another undiscovered continent existed six or seven hundred leagues due west of the Chilean coast. They surmised that a "sandy island" reported by a certain Captain Davis lay off this continent. Roggeveen's instructions were to search for the sandy island and the continent beyond.

In obedience to his instructions, after leaving Easter Island Roggeveen sailed west but found no more islands. On returning home he was accused of having failed in his quest and of brutality toward the natives. For a century and a half more, until his narrative was resurrected by the Hakluyt Society in England, the importance of his discovery was thoroughly underrated, particularly by the Hollanders, who felt they had been throwing good money after bad.

EXTRACT FROM THE OFFICIAL LOG

OF

MR JACOB ROGGEVEEN;

RELATING TO HIS

DISCOVERY OF EASTER ISLAND.

LOG, relating to the voyage to the unknown portion of the World, lying in the South-Sea to the westward of America, done and kept by Mr Jacob Roggeveen, as Commander in Chief of the three Ships: the AREND, whose Captain is Jan Koster, mounted with 32 pieces of Cannon, manned with 110 Persons, and 120 feet in length: the Ship THIENHOVEN, commanded by Capⁿ Cornelis Bouman, being mounted with 24 pieces of Cannon, 80 Persons, and 100 feet in length: together with the Ship DE AFRI-KAANSCHE GALEY, having (blank) pieces of Cannon, 33 men, and 92 feet long, each one being victualled for 28 months, all equipped and fitted out by the Amsterdam Chamber, in pursuance of a Resolution of the Honourable the Directors of the Netherlands chartered West-India Company, adopted at a Meeting of their Board held at The Hague on the 10th of April, Anno 1721.

April

1. Found ourselves at noon in 26 degrees 56 minutes South latitude, and in the longitude by reckoning of 268 degrees 45 minutes, the course was West, the wind East-South-East and South-East, with a topgallant-sail breeze, also light airs to calm. The North-Easterly variation was 2 degrees 18 minutes.

2. The lat. was 27 degrees 31 minutes by reckoning, the long. 268 degrees 23 minutes, corrected course Sou'-Sou'-West 1/2 West, distance 10 miles, the wind Southerly and West-Nor'-West, from calm to a reefed-topsail breeze, with showers, and a thick,

lowering atmosphere. Made a signal for a consultation with the captains of the ships THIENHOVEN and THE AFRICAN GALLEY, of which the resolution adopted is the following:—

COUNCIL of the Officers of the three Ships sailing in company; holden on board the Ship AREND, in the presence of MR JACOB ROGGEVEEN, President; Captain JAN KOSTER, commanding the Ship AREND; Captain CORNELIS BOUMAN, commanding the Ship THIENHOVEN, and Captain ROELOF ROSEN-DAAL, in charge of the Ship THE AFRICAN GALLEY.

Thursday, 2 April, 1722

"The President having pointed out that we have now come about 500 miles to the Westward of Copayapo, situated on the coast of Chile, also that having reached the latitude of 26 degrees 56 minutes South, and yet not come in sight of the unknown Southland (according to existing accounts of it), for the discovery of which our Expedition and Voyage is specially undertaken; moreover, as fortune has not yet favored us with the aforesaid sight, possibly because it lies farther to the Westward than its discoverers reckoned; seeing that they must have been as much liable to error as the most experienced and intelligent experts in seamanship, when sailing along a given parallel on a course from East to West, be it North or South of the Line; therefore the President submits this question to the Council as being a thing of utmost importance, namely, whether it be not judged safest to continue on a West course long enough to feel sure that Copayapo lies fully six hundred miles away to the Eastward of our position, in order thus to follow out and exactly fulfil the intention of our Principals (in accordance with the Instructions issued to us, which lay down and limit the Longitude at 600 miles). All the which, being well considered, it is unanimously approved and agreed upon, after the different longitude of each commander was noted and the mean departure worked out, which was found to be 29 degrees 30 minutes, to sail another degree and 30 minutes farther to the Westward, in order thus to give full effect to the Resolution adopted on March the 15th last: and, further, to continue on the same due West course until one shall have sailed a good

8

clear hundred miles farther, as to wholly obey the aforesaid Instructions in all their particulars in accordance with the dictates
of right and of our duty. So resolved and determined in the Ship
and on the day above stated. (Signed) JACOB ROGGEVEEN,
JAN KOSTER, CORNELIS BOUMAN, ROELOF ROSEN-
DAAL."

4. Reckoned ourselves to be in lat. 27 degrees 1 minute S., and
long. 267 degrees 2 minutes; the course was West, 6 1/2 miles, the
wind between Sou'-Sou'-West and East, with light airs and calms,
and very fine weather, although the sky was overcast; we were able
nevertheless to get two observations of the sun at rising and
setting from which we found the variation to be 2 degrees 37
minutes North-Easterly.

5. Our lat. by reckoning was 27 degrees 4 minutes South and
the long. 266 degrees 31 minutes, course West 1/2 South, distance
7 miles, the wind Nor'-Nor'-West to Sou'-West, breeze unsteady,
with calms, also thick weather and showers. Saw a turtle, floating
weed, and birds. About the 10th glass in the afternoon watch
THE AFRICAN GALLEY, which was sailing ahead of us, lay
to wait for us, making the signal of land in sight; when we came
up with her, after four glasses had run out, for the breeze was
light, we asked what they had seen. On this we were answered
that they had all very distinctly seen a low and flattish island lying
away to starboard, about 5 1/2 miles off, to the nor'ard and
west'ard. Hereupon it was deemed well to stand on under easy
sail to the end of the first watch, and then to lie to and await
the dawn. This being decided, the necessary information was given
to Captain BOUMAN, who was astern; and to the land the
name of Paasch Eyland, because it was discovered by us on Easter
Day. There was great rejoicing among the people and everyone
hoped that this low land might prove to be a foretoken of the
coastline of the unknown Southern continent.

6. Had a light breeze out of the South-East, and East-South-
East, Paasch Eyland lying West by North 8 to 9 miles from us.
Laid our course between West by South and North-West, in
order to run under the lee of the Island, and so avoid the dangers
of a lee shore. At noon the corrected course was West, distance
10 miles, lat. by reckoning 27 degrees 4 minutes South, and long.
265 degrees 42 minutes. In the ninth glass of the afternoon we

saw smoke rising in several places from which we concluded that
there were people dwelling on the same. We therefore thought it
would be well to consider with the Captains of the other ships
whether it were not needful to undertake an expedition ashore,
to the end that we might gain a fitting knowledge of the interior
of the country. On this, it was decided that both the shallops of
the Ships AREND and THIENHOVEN, well manned and
armed, should proceed inshore, and find out a convenient place
for landing a party from the boats, and also to take soundings.
This decision being come to, we stood off and on for the night
with our Ships. Which Resolution is as follows:—

COUNCIL of the Commanders of the three Ships sailing in
company held on board the AREND, in the presence of the un-
dersigned.

Monday the 6th of April, 1722

"The President submitting that we had now arrived within a
distance of some two miles of the Sandy Island, the which lies in
an Easterly direction from the stretch of coast (as yet out of
sight) which is one of the objects of this Expedition to discover,
and as we had seen smoke ascending in several places, from which
it may reasonably be concluded that the aforementioned Island,
although it may be shown to be sandy and barren, has nevertheless
human inhabitants; now, therefore the President moves that it
would be culpable to proceed in a careless and negligent manner,
and that we should stand off and on for to-night with our ships,
and that on the arrival of daylight we send close in to the land
two well manned shallops, properly armed (that we may be in a
state of defence in case of any hostile meeting), and show all
friendliness towards the inhabitants, endeavoring to see and in-
quire what they wear or make use of either as ornaments or for
other purposes, also whether any refreshments in the way of green
stuff, fruit, or beasts can be procured by barter. Which motion
having been discussed, the same is by common assent approved
and adopted: and it is farther decided that both the shallops of the
Ships AREND and THIENHOVEN, shall proceed at daybreak,
and that THE AFRICAN GALLEY should follow as close to

the land as possible and prudent, covering and defending the said shallops (should need arise). Resolved and attested in the said Ship and on the day above mentioned. (Signed): JACOB ROGGEVEEN, JAN KOSTER, CORNELIS BOUMAN, ROELOF ROSENDAAL."

7. The weather was very variable, with thunder, sheet lightning and showers. The wind unsteady from the North West, and occasional calms, so that our shore expedition could not be undertaken with any prospect of success. During the forenoon Captain BOUMAN brought an Easter Islander on board, together with his craft, in which he had come off close to the Ship from the land; he was quite nude, without the slightest covering for that which modesty shrinks from revealing. This hapless creature seemed to be very glad to behold us, and showed the greatest wonder at the build of our Ship. He took special notice of the tautness of our spars, the stoutness of our rigging and running gear, the sails, the guns—which he felt all over with minute attention—and with everything else that he saw; especially when the image of his own features was displayed before him in a mirror, seeing the which, he started suddenly back and then looked towards the back of the glass, apparently in the expectation of discovering there the cause of the apparition.

After we had sufficiently beguiled ourselves with him, and he with us, we started him off again in his canoe towards the shore, having presented him with two strings of blue beads round his neck, a small mirror, a pair of scissors, and other like trifles, which seemed to have a special attraction for him.

But when we had approached within a short distance of the land we saw distinctly that the account of the Sandy and Low Island (so described by Captain William Dampier, in accordance with the statement and testimony of Captain Davis, and of the narrator Lionel Wafer, whose log of this and other discoveries the aforesaid Dampier has made known through the press, and inserted as a prominent feature in his book, which comprises all his own travels and voyages) was not in the least in conformity with our find; and that neither could it be the land which the aforementioned discoverers declare to be visible 14 to 16 miles beyond it and stretching away out of sight, being a range of high land, which the said Dampier conjectured might be the extremity of the unknown Southland. That this Easter Island can not be the Sandy Island is clear, from the fact that the sandy one is small, and low; whereas Easter Island, on the contrary, extends some 15 or 16 miles in circuit, and has at its Eastern and Western points—which lie about five miles from each other—two high hills sloping gradually down, with three or four other smaller hills about their bases which rise above the plain, so that this land is of moderate elevation, and raised above the force of the sea.

The reason why, at first, when at a farther distance off, we had regarded the said Easter Island as being of a sandy nature is that we mistook the parched-up grass, and hay or other scorched and charred brushwood for a soil of that arid nature, because from its outward appearance it suggested no other idea than that of an extraordinarily sparse and meagre vegetation; and the discoverers had consequently bestowed upon it the term sandy.

It may therefore be concluded, in the light of the foregoing explanation, that this Easter Island now discovered will turn out to be some other land lying further to the Eastward than that which is one of the objectives of our Expedition: or else, the discoverers must stand convicted of a whole bundle of lies in their reports, told by word of mouth as well as in writing.

8. We had the wind South, South by East, and Sou'-Sou'-West, with a reefed topsail breeze, unsteady. After breakfast had been served, our shallop was well manned and armed, and likewise the shallop of the Ship THIENHOVEN, now close in with the land; and having received their orders, they reported that the inhabitants there were very finely clad in some stuffs of all kinds of colours, and that they made many signs that we should come on shore, but as our orders were not to do so, if the Indians should be present in large numbers, that was not permitted. Furthermore, some thought they had seen the natives to have plates of silver in their ears, and mother-of-pearl shells as ornaments about their necks. By sundown, having come into the roadstead, between the Ships THIENHOVEN and THE AFRICAN GALLEY, which had already brought to in readiness for us, we let go our anchor in 22 fathoms, coral bottom, at the distance of a quarter of a mile from the beach; the Eastern point of the Island bearing East by South, and the West point West-Nor'-West from us.

9. A great many canoes came off to the ships; these people

showed us at that time their great cupidity for every thing they saw; and were so daring that they took the seamen's hats and caps from off their heads, and sprang overboard with the spoil; for they are surpassingly good swimmers as would seem from the great numbers of them who came swimming off from the shore to the ships. There was also an Easter Islander who climbed in through the cabin window of THE AFRICAN GALLEY, from his canoe, and seeing on the table, a cloth with which it was covered, and deeming it to be a good prize, he made his escape with it there and then; so that one must take special heed to keep close watch over everything. Furthermore, a shore party of 134 men was organized to make investigations for the purpose of reporting upon our mission.

10. In the morning we proceeded with three boats and two shallops, manned by 134 persons, all armed with musket, pistols, and cutlass; on reaching the shore the boats and shallops kept close together in order to lay down their grapnels, leaving twenty men in them, armed as above, to take care of them; THE AFRICAN GALLEY'S boat, was mounted besides with two carronades in the bows. Having seen to all these arrangements, we proceeded in open order, but keeping well together, and clambered over the rocks, which are very numerous on the sea margin, as far as the level land or flat, making signs with the hand that the natives, who pressed round us in great numbers, should stand out of our way and make room for us. Having got so far, a *corps de bataille* was formed up of all the seamen of the three ships, the Commodore, Captains KOSTER, BOUMAN and ROSENDAAL leading, each at the head of his own crew. This column, three ranks in width, occupying a position to the rear of the others, was covered by one half the soldiers under the command of Lieutenant NICOLAAS THONNAR, constituting the right wing; and the left, made up of the other half of the military, was led by Mr. MARTINUS KEERENS, Ensign. After thus disposing our forces we marched forward a little, to make room for some of our people who were behind, that they might fall in with the ranks, who were accordingly halted to allow the hindmost to come up, when, quite unexpectedly and to our great astonishment, four or five shots were heard in our rear, together with a vigorous shout of "'t is tyd, 't is tyd, geeft vuur," ("It's time, it's time, fire!")

13

On this, as in a moment, more than thirty shots were fired, and the Indians, being thereby amazed and scared, took to flight, leaving 10 or 12 dead, besides the wounded. The leaders of the party, standing in front, prevented those in advance from firing on the fugitives; demanding, moreover, who had given the order to shoot, and what had induced him to do so? After a little while the assistant pilot of the ship THIENHOVEN came up to me saying, that he, with six other men, was the hindmost of the party; that, on one of the natives laying hold of the muzzle of his piece to snatch it from him, he struck him a blow; and, further, that another Indian had attempted to strip the jacket off one of the seamen, and that some of the natives seeing our men resist, picked up stones, using threatening gestures as if to pelt us with them, whereby, from all appearance, the firing on the part of my small troop was brought about, although he declared that until then he had given no orders of the least kind. This was, however, no time for hearing other versions of the affair, and that much had to be deferred till a better opportunity. After the astonishment and terror of the natives were somewhat allayed, on their seeing that our hostilities were not persisted in, they were given to know by signs that the victims had threatened to make an assault upon us by stone-throwing, and the inhabitants, who had been just in front of us all the time, approached our leaders again; in particular one who seemed to be in authority over the other headmen, for, giving a general direction that everything they had should be fetched and laid before us, including fruit, root crops, and poultry, the order was promptly obeyed with reverence and bowing by those round about, as the event proved; for in a little while they brought a great abundance of sugar-cane, fowls, yams, and bananas; but we gave them to understand through signs that we desired nothing, excepting only the fowls, which were about sixty in number, and thirty bunches of bananas, for which we paid them ample value in striped linen, with which they appeared to be well pleased and satisfied. By the time we had fully investigated things, and especially their cloth stuffs and the dyes of them, and also the supposed silver plates and mother-of-pearl, it was found that they were made up of pieces patched together; that is, that the wraps worn on their bodies were composed of some field-product, sewn three or four ply in thickness, yet neat and trim, which material (as called in the West Indies) is a sort of Piet: further, that the soil of the country (as we saw in several places) was red, and yellowish, into the which when mixed with water they dip their garments and afterwards let them dry, which shows that their dye is not fast, for when felt about and handled one finds the colour comes off on one's fingers, not only after touching new articles but also from old and worn ones. The plates imagined to be of silver were made out of the root of some vegetable,—as one might say in Holland, of good stout parsnips or carrots. This ear-ornament is roundish, or oval, having a diameter of about two inches measured through the widest section, and one and a half inches measured across the lesser; being three inches, at a guess, in length. To understand how these supposed silver plates are fixed in the ears as ornaments one must know that the lobes of these people's ears are stretched, from their youth up; and their centre is slit open, in such wise that the lesser rim of the plug, being stuck through the opening in the lobe, is then pushed on towards the thicker end, which accordingly faces towards the front, and completely stuffs the opening. Furthermore, the mother-of-pearl which was seen as a neck pendant is a flat shell of the same tint as the inner lip of our oysters. When these Indians go about any job which might set their earplugs waggling, and bid fair to do them any hurt, they take them out and hitch the rim of the lobe up over the top of the ear, which gives them a quaint and laughable appearance! These people have well proportioned limbs, with large and strong muscles; they are big in stature, and their natural hue is not black, but pale yellow or sallowish, as we saw in the case of many of the lads, either because they had not painted their bodies with dark blue, or because they were of superior rank and had consequently no need to labour in the field. These people have also snow-white teeth, with which they are exceptionally well provided, even the old and hoary, as was evidenced by the cracking of a large and hard nut, whose shell was thicker and more resisting than our peach stones. The hair of their heads, and the beards of most of them, were short, although others wore it long, and hanging down the back, or plaited and coiled on the top of the head in a tress, like the Chinese at Batavia, which is there termed conde. What the form of worship of these people comprises we were not able to gather any full knowledge of, owing to the shortness of our stay among them; we noticed only that they kindle fire in front of certain remarkably tall stone figures they set up; and, thereafter squatting on their heels with heads bowed down, they bring the palms of their hands together and alternately raise and lower them. At first, these stone figures caused us to be filled with wonder, for we could not understand how it was possible that people who are destitute of heavy or thick timber, and also of stout cordage, out of which to construct gear, had been able to erect them; nevertheless some of these statues were a good 30 feet in height and broad in proportion. This perplexity ceased, however, with the discovery, on removing a piece of the stone, that they were formed out of clay or some kind of rich earth, and that small smooth flints had been stuck over afterwards, which are fitted very closely and neatly to each other, so as to make up the semblance of a human figure. Moreover, one saw reaching downwards from the shoulders a slight elevation or prominence which represented the arms, for all the statues seem to convey the idea that they were hung about with a long robe from the neck right down to the soles of the feet. They have on the head a basket heaped up with flints painted white deposited in it. It was incomprehensible to us how these people cook their food, for no one was able to perceive or find that they had any earthen pots, pans, or vessels. The only thing which appeared to us was that they scrape holes in the ground with their hands, and lay large and small flint pebbles in them (for we saw no other kinds of stone): then, having got dried litter from the fields and laid over the pebbles, they set fire to it and in a little time brought us a boiled fowl to eat very neatly wrapped round in a kind of rush, clean and hot. Though they were thanked by means of signs, we had quite enough business in hand to look after our people so as to keep order among them, and prevent any affront being offered; and also that in the event of any struggle occurring they should not allow themselves to be taken by surprise, for although these people showed us every sign of friendship, yet the experience of others has taught us that one may not put too much trust in any Indians, as recounted in the Journal of the Nassau Fleet, which lost seventeen men on one occasion through the willingness of the natives of Terra de Feu to pretend to be well disposed.

We then, being baulked from making any sufficiently detailed inquiry, concluded that they must have large hollow flint-stones under the soil, which hold water when they set about boiling anything, and that afterwards they arch it over with stones on which to light the fire, and thus boil their food by means of the heat thrown downwards, until tender. It is also very remarkable that we saw no more than two or three old women, those were wearing a garment reaching from the waist down to below their knees, and another slung on the shoulders: yet so that the skin covering their pendant breasts was bare. But young women and lasses did not come forward amongst the crowd, so that one must believe the jealousy of the men had moved them to hide them away in some distant place in the island. Their houses or huts are without any ornamentation, and have a length of fifty feet and a width of fifteen: the height being nine feet, as it appeared by guess. The construction of the walls, as we saw in the framework of a new building, is begun with stakes which are stuck into the ground and secured straight upright, across which other long strips of wood which I may call laths are lashed, to the height of four or five, thus completing the framework of the building. Then the interstices, which are all of oblong shape, are closed up and covered over with a sort of rush or long grass, which they put on very thickly, layer upon layer, and fasten on the inner side with lashings (the which they know how to make from a certain field product called Piet, very neatly and skilfully, and is in no way inferior to our own thin cord); so that they are always as well shut in against wind and rain as those who live beneath thatched roofs in Holland.

These dwellings have no more than one entrance way, which is so low that they pass in creeping on their knees, being round above, as a vault or archway; the roof is also of the same form. All the chattels we saw before us (for these long huts admit no daylight except through the one entrance-way, and are destitute of windows and closely shut in all round) were mats spread on the floor, and a large flint stone which many of them use for a pillow. Furthermore they had round about their dwellings certain big blocks of hewn stone, three or four feet in breadth, and fitted together in a singularly neat and even manner; and, according to our judgment, these serve them for a stoop on which to sit and chat during the cool of the evening. It only remains to say, in concluding the subject of these dwelling-huts, that we did not see more than six or seven of them at the place where we landed, from which it may clearly be inferred that all the Indians make use of their possessions in common, for the large size and small number of their dwellings give one to know that many live together and sleep in a single building; but if one should therefore conclude that the women are held in common among them, one must naturally expect depravity and bickering to ensue.

Finally, as to their seagoing craft, they are of poor and flimsy construction; for their canoes are fitted together of a number of small boards and light frames, which they skilfully lace together with very fine laid twine made from the above-mentioned vegetable product Piet. But as they lack the knowledge, and especially the material, for caulking the great number of seams of their canoes, and making them tight, they consequently leak a great deal; on account of which they are necessitated to spend half their time in baling. Their canoes are about ten feet long, not counting the high and pointed stem and stern pieces. Their width is such that, with their legs packed close together, they can just sit in them so as to paddle ahead.

It was now deemed advisable to go to the other side of the Island, whereto the King or Head Chief invited us, as being the principal place of their plantations and fruit-trees, for all the things they brought to us of that kind were fetched from that quarter,—inasmuch as the Northerly wind which began to blow made our anchorage a leeshore: the more so because we had not many people on board the Ships, who could get help from us if necessary in the event of the wind waxing strong; moreover, the boats and shallops being filled to the utmost with men, these would in such a case not have been able to get back on board, either by reason of the heavy sea on the beach or of its becoming impossible for them to row. Therefore it was deemed well to pull off at once in good order, the which was presently put into practice. Having arrived on board we resolved to sail another hundred miles farther to the Westward so that by thus doing we should punctually follow our Instructions and the Resolution adopted in reference to them, in all details; although, before doing so, we should make a short Cruise away down Eastwards, to see whether we could discover the Low and Sandy Island; for, in the event of our finding it, the first portion of our cruise in the South Sea would necessarily terminate, as having accomplished its purpose: the contents of which Resolution are:—

COUNCIL of the Commanders of the three Ships sailing in company, held on board the Ship AREND, when the Shore Expedition had been despatched and accomplished with three boats and two shallops, well armed and manned.

Friday the 10th of April, 1722

"The President have called together the Commanders of this Expedition, to the end that each one should submit his ideas and opinions concerning the newly found Island, namely, whether in view of this discovery the Resolution considered and adopted by this Council on the 2nd inst. should be punctually observed and fulfilled: or whether, on the contrary, we should proceed on our course another hundred miles Westwards, inasmuch as this land discovered (being called by us Paasch Eyland, because it was sighted and discovered on Easter Day) can not be said to be a small, low, and sandy Island, covering as it does an extent of sixteen Dutch miles in circuit and being fairly high land, the which was lying 8 or 9 miles away from us when THE AFRICAN GALLEY made the signal of land in sight. As this distance may with safety be deemed correct, seeing that it took us the whole of the following day with a fresh breeze blowing, to get within a couple of miles or so by eventide. Nor can the aforementioned land be termed sandy, because we found it not only not sandy but on the contrary exceedingly fruitful, producing bananas, potatoes, sugar-cane of remarkable thickness, and many other kinds of the fruits of the earth; although destitute of large trees and domestic animals, except poultry. This place, as far as its rich soil and good climate are concerned, is such that it might be made into an earthly Paradise, if it were properly worked and cultivated; which is now only done in so far as the inhabitants are obliged to for the maintenance of life. And furthermore, it is quite improper to give this discovery the name of a range of high land; if one supposes that by ill luck we sailed by the Low and Sandy Island without seeing it, the which is not probable, as our course was directed in such wise that we should inevitably have sighted it if so be that this Easter Island is the land which is described as being a range of high land. Therefore one may conclude with good reason that this Easter Island is some other land than any we are seeking, and that one part of our voyage is made good; since it fails to present those characteristics which belong to the land we hoped to meet with. The President submits all the above remarks to this Council for consideration, in order to avail himself of its opinions as may be proper.

"Whereupon, all these points being attentively noted and maturely weighed, it is unanimously resolved that, indisputably, the above-mentioned Easter Island does not in the least conform to the description of a range of high land, being of only moderate elevation; that, also, it is absolutely impossible that the finer metals should occur here, as we learned by experience from ocular inspection, that the Inhabitants are without any such, and employ as coverings and ornaments only certain produce of vegetable origin; and that they understand sewing these handsomely and neatly together three or four ply in thickness for the sake of warmth and strength. Furthermore that they plait together as ornaments some feathers of the domestic fowl (of which last very few were seen, however) so as to form a circlet worn on the head, and the painting of their faces, and other parts of the body as well, with regular and well proportioned designs after such a manner that one side of the body is in conformity with the other, also some flat shells worn as neck ornaments, and the slit in the ear-lobes plugged with some kind of root (shaped like our parsnips) for adorning the ears. Further, that we have not seen the small, low and sandy Island which must be the outlier and true sign of that land we are in search of; therefore it is by unanimous assent agreed upon and declared that we continue the course West along the parallel of 27 degrees of South latitude until we shall have sailed another hundred miles, and on arrival there, we are to be guided by circumstances and to take such action as may then be deemed proper.

"So resolved in the Ship and on the day above stated. (Signed) JACOB ROGGEVEEN, JAN KOSTER, CORNELIS BOUMAN, ROELOF ROSENDAAL."

This resolution being carried and signed, Captain JAN KOSTER suggested by way of discussion, that it should be a very easy and simple matter to ascertain whether the above-mentioned Easter Island is really the land we are aiming after and towards which we have directed our course, if we were now to make only a short Cruise by sailing 12 miles Eastwards, and that the Ships should keep two miles apart from each other, but at the same time resume close company if it should happen that a low and sandy Island should be sighted, which would establish the truth that the aforesaid Easter Island is the land we have been minded to discover. And in case we get no view of the said Sandy Island that then also the before-named Easter Island must of necessity be some other land (although lying right in our track) than that towards which our Expedition is directed. Furthermore, that if the Sandy Island should be discovered, a Northerly course should be shaped in order to get into the steadier and stronger trade-wind, for the furthering of the second item in our Voyage: since the first would fulfil itself, and thereby terminate, on our meeting with the Sandy Island before mentioned. All the which being considered, was approved and adopted by common assent.

"So resolved and determined in the Ship and on the day of the foregoing Resolution. (Signed) JACOB ROGGEVEEN, JAN KOSTER, CORNELIS BOUMAN, ROELOF ROSEN-DAAL."

11. The wind this day was Nor'-Nor'-West and Nor'-West, with a topsail-breeze and rough sea. We laid out the best bower, and sent down the fore and main yards. About the fourth glass of the first watch the Ship THIENHOVEN's working cable parted; and being hailed to know if she wanted assistance, they answered 'No.'

12. The working cable of THE AFRICAN GALLEY carried away about dawn, through which misfortune both Ships got so much nearer the beach before they were brought up by another anchor, that if they had then dragged, or the cable had parted a second time, they would inevitably have suffered shipwreck: for, as there was not time enough to sheet their sails home by the wind, the Ship or both Ships would have foundered against the rocks, by reason of the strength of the wind and the heavy rollers setting shorewards. The danger of the other ships caused us to

decide to get a spring on our own cable, so as to be able to fill
our sails in case of emergency, and be ready to claw off the lee
shore and thus endeavor to save the ship and ourselves: to which
end we swayed our yards aloft again so as to be all ready to put
to sea whenever needs should demand. But the wind shifting
with a rain squall from the Nor'-West to West, saved us from this
extreme measure. We all weighed our anchors, therefore, and
made sail together; with the setting of the sun, the East point
of the Island bearing Sou'-West by South, and the West point
Sou'-West by West, six miles distant.

13. We were in the latitude by observation 27 degrees 7 minutes South, and the longitude 265 degrees 56 minutes by reckoning; the corrected course was South-East, 4 1/2 miles, the wind
between Nor'-Nor'-West and South by East, with unsteady airs
and rain squalls. After Easter Island bore West by North from
us, we steered due East, the weather being very bright and clear
all the while. When we had left the land so far behind that it
could scarcely be made out from the mast-head, we sailed on
another three miles farther notwithstanding, in order to be quite
certain of covering the whole distance between the Sandy Island
and Easter Island; but, not sighting the same, we decided to
wear ship in order to proceed on our voyage to the Westward.
We therefore signalled our consorts to alter their course, and to
steer West, expressing our hope that a good discovery of a high
and wide-stretching tract of land should result after a little while.

III

THE VICEROY NAMES
THE ISLAND: SAN CARLOS

In the last spurt of energy of the Spanish Empire under Carlos III, the only one of the late Bourbons who had any brains, the Viceroy of Peru, Don Manuel de Amat, was instructed to send out an expedition in search of the island, known to the Spaniards as Davis Island, referred to by various British navigators and visited a half century before by Jacob Roggeveen, whose narrative was carefully conserved in the Archives of the Indies in Seville. Byron's and Wallis's cruises in the central Pacific had made the Spanish authorities nervous about further encroachments on their lifeline to Manila.

Don Manuel promptly fitted out the fullrigged ship *San Lorenzo* and the frigate *Rosalía* for an expedition to the westward. They sailed from Callao in the fall of 1770 and after five weeks were in the latitude of Easter Island.

Early in the following year they returned to an anchorage behind the island of Chiloé off the Chilean coast and the Viceroy was able to write the Secretary of State for the Indies that the mission was accomplished. The inhabitants of the island of San Carlos had proved peaceable and friendly. They did not resemble Indians in any way. If they had worn clothes they would have looked like Europeans. They had accepted His Majesty's sovereignty with signs of rejoicing. He added that he had made sure that there were no English established on the island, or on the coasts of Chile south of Concepción. He included in his dispatches several narratives by members of the expedition describing their visits ashore.

THE NARRATIVE
OF DON FELIPE GONZALEZ Y HAEDO,
CAPTAIN OF THE SAN LORENZO

On the 14th of November 1770 we found ourselves, at half-past seven in the morning with very little wind, and made a signal to the frigate for her captain and such officers as could be spared to come on board of us which, however, they asked permission to defer until after they had breakfasted; when we all, from both vessels, assembled together in the chief cabin. Our Commodore then directed, in the presence of all, that the instructions and commands which he held from the Viceroy be read aloud by the paymaster of this ship, which was done. He then stated, before all, that although his orders only required him to go as far as long. 264° yet nevertheless he was minded to continue on while so many birds remained in sight, and that he had called us all together in order that we should communicate our views to him. All agreed in the Commodore's opinion, since it coincided with their own. At half-past two in the afternoon those of the frigate returned on board of her, and we resumed our course as before.

On this same day, at six in the evening, some sandpipers appeared. These birds are accustomed to fly no more than about fifteen leagues from land; and we remained hove to for the night.

On the 15th at five in the morning we made all sail, and at seven o'clock we sighted an island to the N.W. of us, from 8 to 10 leagues distant. We headed for it, and upon finding ourselves within some three leagues of its Eastern coast we saw it to be all bold and rock-bound, on account of which at noon we decided to bear up for the Northern side and see whether we might find any harbour round there. At this time our position was ascertained by observation to be in lat. 27° 15′ S. and long. 264° 20′, so that the other point should be in 27° 06′ of lat. South, and therefore 34° 10′ to the westward of the meridian of Callao, measured by the arc, or the equivalent of a chord of 30° 30′. On this island we bestowed the name of San Carlos, being that of the reigning king.

. . . On the 15th, after bearing up at noon in quest of a harbour on the north side of the island we noticed, as we closed in with the land, that there were people on shore who were making signals to us by means of smoke, in several parts of this new land; and when we had rounded the north-easternmost point, called after San Felipe, we saw a bay which appeared might prove a good harbour, being then about half a league distant; and we lowered a boat into the water. I embarked in her with Don Alberto Lesuda, Captain of Marines, a serjeant, six men, the boat duly equipped, and all hands provided with their respective arms, proceeding with the precaution and care appropriate to the business in hand.

We went in to take soundings of the bay without being acquainted with the character of the natives, or whether they possessed canoes or not. We left the ship at a quarter past three in the afternoon, and proceeded to take soundings shorewards. We got no bottom until quite close in, where I found thirty fathoms; and from thence to the beach a very foul bottom of rocks, gravel, and coral; from thirty to forty fathoms I found coarse sand, but with a few large round stones; this might serve nevertheless for a short time, while searching for a better anchorage.

At the time we set about taking soundings the frigate's boat came along for the same purpose, in which was Don Buenaventura Moreno, Captain of Marines, similarly armed and equipped; and when we drew close in to the shore taking soundings, we saw several natives of the country on the beach shouting to us in their language, of which we understood nothing. These were naked, and painted, body and face. When I had made an examination of the bottom I returned on board my ship, and the other boat to hers: I explained the quality of the ground to the Commodore, and having arrived somewhere about 6 o'clock in the evening he decided not to move away from the place until the following day.

On the 16th at half-past five in the morning I started away from the ship's side in the cutter, and proceeded to take up a position where the boat anchorage was, to serve as a mark for the ship, which came in and let go in 35 1/2 fathoms, coarse sand; and having laid out another anchor in 50 fathoms, she swung to with 28 under the keel, same bottom. The leading marks for this position are the small saddle-shaped hill bearing S. 3° W., with Cape San Lorenzo E. 1/4 S.E. 3° E. by the needle, which in this locality has 3° variation N.E.

While acting as a beacon as above stated and awaiting the arrival of the ship, three of the natives swam off, painted in various colours, and keeping near the boat, shouting constantly, until one of them came at last so close as to present me with a morsel of yam: I gave him some biscuit and tobacco, all of which he accepted. He carried his provisions in a satchel neatly plaited of fine straw. When the ship came to an anchor these three went off ashore again, but returned with another, swimming and making straight for the ship, on board of which they climbed with much agility, shouting all the while and exhibiting much gayness of spirit. They ran about freely from stem to stern, and full of mirth, climbing about the rigging like sailormen. Our people played the bagpipes and fife to them, and they began to dance, evincing great pleasure. They were given ribbons, shirts, trousers, seamen's jumpers, and small gilt metal crosses: they accepted them all with gladness, the biscuit they received without remark until they saw our people eat some. It pleased them well and then they asked for it, and applied themselves freely to the consumption of salt pork and rice, &c.

On the said 16th of November we embarked at one o'clock in the day, Don Cayetano Lángara, senior lieutenant, Don Pedro Obregon, midshipman, a serjeant, a corporal of marines, a gunner, some marines and myself, in the launch, fully armed and equipped for service, with orders to make a complete circuit of the island in company with the *Rosalía's* launch, with her officer Don Demetrio Ezeta, senior lieutenant, each one fitted with a swivel gun in the bows. We set to work to take soundings, giving names to the points, bays, &c., as shown on the plan of the island. At half-past six in the evening we brought to in a cove which we called after Lángara: we tried to effect a landing but this was not practicable as the sea was breaking with such force all along the shore, which was rocky at all points; and during the remainder of the day the only place we found fit to land at was the cove of San Juan, as it had a sandy beach. We did not disclose our presence there, in order not to lose time. We considered that it must have a plentiful supply of fresh water, because we saw there more gravel than in any other part of the island. We also found the best anchorage for ships.

On the 17th day dawned with the horizon clear, and a moderate breeze from the Eastward. At five in the morning we got under way in both launches and made sail towards the Cape of San Antonio. Half a league before reaching the cape we came abreast of a point, off which were a quantity of rocks or boulders sticking up out of the water; and saw that two little canoes were coming out from among them with two men in each, making for the *Santa Rosalía*'s launch; so we waited for them in order that they might join our party. They gave the people of the said launch plantains, Chili peppers, sweet potatoes and fowls; and in return our men gave them hats, *chamorretas* [trinkets], &c., and they went off contentedly with these to the shore. These canoes are constructed of five extremely narrow boards (on account of there being no thick timber in the country) about a span in width; they are consequently so crank that they are provided with an outrigger to prevent them from capsizing; and I think that these are the only ones in the whole of the island. They are fitted together with wooden pegs in place of nails. Then we passed on to examine the rocky islets to which we gave the name of Lángara: they lie s.w. 1/4 s. from the cape of San Cristoval, the seaward one being about a mile off that headland, and the inshore one in between. They are about half a cable apart the one from the other, and we found 26 fathoms there, rocky bottom. The middle one resembles a high church tower; we attempted to gain a footing on it, but found it little accessible. We passed on to the outer one, where we succeeded in landing, and on which we found two large masses of seaweed, many black flints, some sea urchins and small crabs, eggs of sea-gulls and their fledgelings. On these rocks alone did we see any sea-gulls, and excepting domestic fowls we saw no other kind of birds on either of the other islets, nor on the island of San Carlos, either small or large, wild or domesticated. The islanders breed these fowls in little runs scraped out in the ground and thatched over.

Having made an investigation of these islets we pursued our

course along the coast, at times under sail, at other times under oars; and, the wind holding contrary, at three o'clock in the afternoon we stood in towards a smooth patch of foreshore about a league away to the N.E. of Cape San Francisco. Here we decided to bring up for the night in a small bay which appeared to us to be a suitable place for the purpose and to which we gave the appellation of the cave, because there was one adjoining the beach at this place with furrows in it of various tints, from which the natives gave us to understand by signs they obtained the pigments with which they paint themselves. This bay is only suitable for launches. We all went ashore to eat our dinner, which we carried with us for that purpose, and some hundred or so natives came to look on, offering us fruits and hens. The officer, Don Cayetano de Lángara, issued orders to our people that no one, under pain of a severe flogging, should accept any article from the islanders without giving some equivalent in return, or something of greater value than that which they received, since it was certain there was disposition to exchange articles; which was immediately put into practice.

When we sat down to eat we noticed that they all withdrew, and that only one remained, as if to watch; I ordered my servant to give this one a little cooked rice and salt pork, all of which he ate and found much to his taste. When we had finished dinner we betook ourselves for a stroll on the island: our people were again warned to do no injury to the natives nor to their plantations. When we had walked up the slope of the beach we found all those whom we had previously seen, and we passed over in a body without saying anything to them until they, putting aside their shyness, came close up to our people and conducted us to see a long dwelling-house which was about a quarter of a league off. This house was 27 paces in length, 2 1/2 yards high at the center, and 1 1/4 yards at the ends, more or less; and at the middle part was a doorway 1 yard in height. It was framed on some six poles of 4 yards long, and a span in thickness. After having shown us this sumptuous edifice, they began to sing and to dance by way of paying us a compliment and being very happy at seeing us. We walked about two leagues, and at that distance (throughout which many islanders accompanied us) we saw a plantain garden which stretched about a quarter of a league in extent, and was about half that distance in breadth. There were other small plantain gardens, and several plantations and fields of sugar-cane, sweet potatoes, taro, yams, white gourds, and plants like those whose leaves are employed at Callao for making mats. We saw a root which they chew and daub their bodies and limbs all over with: it is good for yielding a very fine yellow dye. At dusk we made back to our launches to stay the night, without our peaceful relations with the natives having been in any way disturbed, which may be attributed to the order which the officer gave to our men not to give them any offence, backed by the threat of a flogging, without which our marines and seamen would have destroyed these poor wretches' plantations.

The morning of the 18th broke fine, with the wind from the North: we continued along the coast, which is all surf-bound, sounding as we went. At 8 o'clock the frigate's launch, not being able to make any headway against the wind, put into a small bay to wait for it to calm down; and we ourselves reached the cover of the Bell under oars at 5 in the afternoon, in order to stay there the night. We stepped ashore there and some islanders came to receive us, but a shower of rain made us turn back to our launch for the night. On that side of this cove towards the headland of San Felipe a rock shaped like a bell juts out from the shore, and from this the cove derives its name.

We made sail at daybreak on the 19th with the wind at N. and fine weather, for the headland of San Felipe, where we were joined by the other launch, who reported that they had no news. At this time we were battling with the current, against which we were not able to make any headway with the oars, and which was running to the eastward. The frigate's launch, being smaller than ours, was able to get along better than we, and those on board seeing us contending against the persistence of the current, sent us the cutter with a fresh crew to relieve our men, who were done up. Yet the current made itself felt with such force that after pulling from 9 a.m. until 6 o'clock in the evening we had scarcely made one league of distance from Cape San Felipe. At this hour, however, God favoured us with a thunder squall accompanied by rain and a change of wind from N.W. to S.E., which brought us alongside at half-past seven o'clock, thus terminating our expedition without other adventures than already related.

We were satisfied that the roadstead in which we lay at anchor is the best the whole island affords, excepting that of San Juan, to which we did not remove, as we should so soon be leaving this country again, inasmuch as there only remained for us to take possession of it in the name of the King.

On the 20th, at daybreak, all the seamen bearing arms embarked in the launches and cutters of both vessels, under Don Alberto Olaondo, Captain of Marines, with his party of marines and those from the frigate, who together made up 250 men. All these proceeded towards the interior of the island to survey the country. Our Commander Don José Bustillos, went with another body of marines and seamen, and the two chaplains, who conveyed with them three crosses to be erected on three hill-tops which, as may be seen on the Plan, exist at the N.E. point of the island.

A great number of native inhabitants received them on landing, and offered to assist our officers in the disembarkation, which, in fact, they did; and took charge of the three crosses, which they carried up to the said hills: the chaplains chanting Litanies, and the islanders joining with our people in the responses, *ora pro nobis*. At the moment of digging the hole on the centre hill, a fine spring of fresh water broke out, very good and abundant. The crosses being planted the party fired three volleys of musketry, and the ships replied with twenty-one guns each, to the joyful shout of *Viva el Rey*. The islanders responded with our own people; they pronounce with such ease that they repeat whatever is said to them just like ourselves. This undertaking being achieved we all returned on board.

It need not be said that the islanders were terrified at the noise of the gunfire and musketry: this must happen to people who have not used or seen such inventions.

The women made use of wraps or cloaks: one which covers them from the waist downwards, and another about the breasts. There are others also who wear only a rag or strip of some root, which they place in front like the men. They have several very low and small huts, and some like the one first mentioned.

Throughout the island, but especially near the sea-beach, there are certain huge blocks of stone in the form of the human figure. They are some twelve yards in height, and I think they are their idols. They could not bear to see us smoke cigars: they begged our sailors to extinguish them and they did so. I asked one of them the reason, and he made signs that the smoke went upwards; but I do not know what this meant or what he wished to say.

I fancy that the cloaks or wraps of the said islanders are made from the fibres of stems of the banana plant, which, when dry, they put together as may suit their purpose: it is not woven, but is joined together by strands of the same material which they thread on bone needles of the size of a cloak-maker's needle. They made fishing-lines of this same fibre, as well as nets after the fashion of our small nets; but of little strength.

They have very little wood; but if they were to plant trees there would be no lack of it; and I believe that even the cotton plant would yield, as the country is very temperate: and wheat, garden plants, pot-herbs, &c. They dye their cloaks yellow.

The number of the inhabitants, including both sexes, will be from about nine hundred to a thousand souls: and of these very few indeed are women,—I do not believe they amount to seventy —and but few boys. They are in hue like a quadroon, with smooth hair and short beards, and they in no way resemble the Indians of the South American continent; and if they wore clothing like ourselves they might very well pass for Europeans. They eat very little, and have few needs: they do altogether without liquor of any kind.

On the 21st at noon we put to sea from this Island of Davis: we sailed some 70 leagues to the Westward to see whether any more land lay in that direction.

Declaration

The following attestation is made in obedience to the Official Instructions.

Dn Antonio Romero, Staff Paymaster in the Royal Navy, at present serving on board H.M. Ship of the Line named the Sn Lorenzo.

I certify—that, by direction of Dn Felipe Gonzalez y Haedo, Captain in the Royal Navy, commanding this ship and the Frigate *Sta Rosalía* sailing under her escort, whom the Most Excellent Senor the Viceroy, Governor, and Captain-General of the Kingdom of Peru, Dn Manuel de Amat, under whose orders he is, has appointed for the investigation of this island, commonly marked on the charts by the name of David, it has on the day and date hereof been examined by sea and by land, and there has in so far as is possible been made known to and recognized by its native inhabitants their lawful Sovereign, and his powerful arm for their defence against foreign enemies, the which they have acknowledged with many demonstrations of pleasure and rejoicing. And in testimony of so happy a success three crosses have, by their consent, been erected on the hill which is at the N.E. extremity of the island; and the name of Sn Carlos has been bestowed upon the said island, in the presence of the native inhabitants assembled to the number of 800, and of all the officers, crew, and ship's company told off for the occasion under the command of Dr. Josef Bustillos, Knight of the Order of St. James and a Commander in the Royal Navy. And the which three crosses being set up in position, the litany was sung and at its conclusion a triple salute of musketry was fired by the aforesaid seamen and ship's company, and another of 21 guns by the ship and the Frigate.

And in order that this act of solemn possession may be made known and established by evidence I declare this at the Island of Sn Carlos: the 20th of November, 1770—Dn Antonio Romero."

To this document the chiefs appended signatures in what the Spaniards took to be their own writing.

IV

CAPTAIN COOK'S SHORT VISIT IN 1774

James Cook, the most accomplished of English eighteenth-century navigators, came from very humble beginnings. Raised with little schooling in a Yorkshire village, he was early apprenticed to a Whitby coal merchant. He learned seamanship in the hard school of the Newcastle colliers, with occasional trips across the stormy North Sea to Danish and Norwegian ports. By the age of twenty he was mate on a collier. To escape a pressgang he enlisted in the Royal Navy and rose to the position of Master on the sloop *Grampus*. He must have studied constantly because he was soon entrusted with the survey of the Gulf of St. Lawrence and the coasts of Newfoundland and Labrador. His work was so accurate that he was appointed to the post of Marine Surveyor. His first publication was an account of a solar eclipse. In 1768 he was put in charge of the expedition to observe the transit of Venus. Commissioned Lieutenant on the *Endeavor*, he charted many South Pacific islands, and a large part of the coasts of Australia and of New Zealand.

Returning to England, he was promoted to Commander and sent off again to solve once for all the question of the South Pacific continent. Did it exist or didn't it? He had the services of two firstrate naturalists, the Forsters, father and son, on this cruise. Though already proficient in Pacific navigation, his ships the *Resolution* and *Adventure*

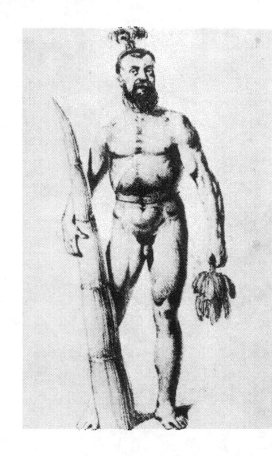

1. Eighteenth-century Easter Island man with totora reed float

2. Eighteenth-century Easter Island woman

3. Easter Island girl wearing
one of the straw hats that
the Frenchmen of La
Pérouse's expedition found
so becoming

4. The Easter Island statues in 1774. From an original oil painting by William Hodges, official draughtsman on Captain Cook's second voyage

5. Watercolor by Pierre Loti: Easter Island group in the mid-
nineteenth century

6. Modern islanders chopping the tuff of a monolith's base with basalt picks in the course of reconstruction work

7. Modern and ancient engineering methods. A crane is added to the cradle the ancient Easter Islanders used to move their monoliths

8. The latest way of restoring
the topknots to the fallen
statues. We still don't know
exactly how they got them
up there originally

9. The great figure at Tahai set back on its pedestal

10. (RIGHT) The fallen statue at Tahai restored with its topknot. The group photograph is of interest because the man in a white monastic gown (left front) is Father Sebastian

12. The megalithic wall at Vinapu

13. Stonework of the earliest type

11. The restored *moai* dominates the shore

14. Orongo: sculptured rocks and the bird islands beyond

15. (RIGHT) Orongo: Mask of Makemake, praying birdmen and the crater lake of Rano Kao beyond

16. **Rano** Kao and the bird islands

17. Orongo

18. Underground dwelling at Orongo

19. Rano Kao crater

20. Ahu Hekii topknots

21. The quarry where they carved
the topknots

22. All over the island the rocks
have been engraved with various
patterns

23. (LEFT) In ancient times totora reed was used for boat building and until the middle nineteenth century for roofing the canoeshaped communal dwellings

24. *Kava kava* figure. These small carved wooden images, said to commemorate the state of desperate starvation in which the first settlers reached the island, were family penates and good luck fetishes. They are still being turned out very acceptably for the tourist trade

25. Ancient head.
It suggests a portrait of Picasso

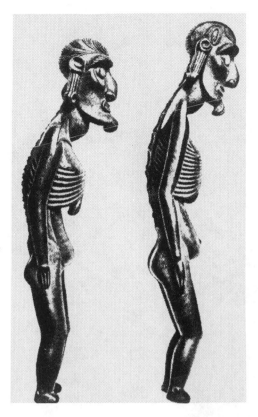

26. Wood carvings:
Kava kava figures

27. Wood carvings:
Kava kava figures

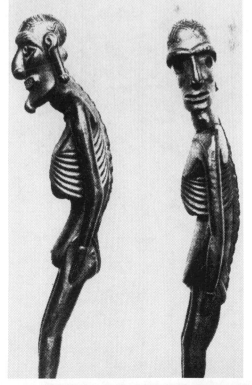

28. Crater lake at Rano Raraku—the rushes are totora reed

were still not smart enough sailers to beat to windward across the southeastern Pacific to Easter Island, which was on his itinerary. He had to sail far into the Antarctic. From there taking advantage of the cold westerlies and the Humboldt current, he made his landfall on Easter Island, like the other European navigators, from the east. Disappointed in his hope of provisions and fresh water, after establishing the exact position of Easter Island on his chart he sailed off after five days toward the more fortunate islands to the westward.

Back in England after his second Pacific cruise he astonished the Admiralty by bringing his entire ship's company—except for one man—home in good health. He had discovered the efficacy of lime juice as a preventive of scurvy.

This time he was awarded appropriate honors. He was given the rank of Post-Captain and elected to the Royal Society. Benjamin Franklin was so impressed by his scientific accomplishments that he urged the commissioners in charge of the new navy of the revolting American colonies to instruct their skippers to do no harm to Captain Cook's ships, now outfitting for a third Pacific expedition.

Having charted a large part of Bering Strait and the Alaskan coast, he met his death almost accidentally on the island of Hawaii. He had landed on the beach in Kealakekua Bay with a shore party which was threatened by a hostile swarm of natives. After ordering his men to retire he remained behind to see that they all made the boats and, turning to follow, was struck down by a blow with a club. The boats' crews helplessly watched his body being hacked to pieces on the shore.

NARRATIVE
FROM CAPTAIN COOK'S
SECOND VOYAGE

I now steered north, inclining to the east, and in the evening we were overtaken by a furious storm at west-south-west, attended with snow and sleet. It came so suddenly upon us, that before we could take in our sails, two old top-sails, which we had bent to the yards were blown to pieces, and the other sails much damaged. The gale lasted, without the least intermission, till the next morning, when it began to abate; it however continued to blow very fresh till noon on the 12th, when it ended in a calm. At this time we were in the latitude of 50° 14′ S., longitude 95° 18′ W. Some birds being about the ship, we took the advantage of the calm to put a boat in the water, and shot several birds, on which we feasted the next day. One of these birds was of that sort which has been so often mentioned in this journal under the name of Port-Egmont hens. They are of the gull kind, about the size of a raven with a dark brown plumage, except the under side of each wing, where there are some white feathers. The rest of the birds were albatrosses and sheerwaters.

After a few hours' calm, having got a breeze at north-west, we made a stretch to the south-west for twenty-four hours; in which route we saw a piece of wood, a bunch of weed, and a living petrel. The wind having veered more to the west, made us tack and stretch to the north till noon on the 14th, at which time we were in the latitude of 49° 32′ S., longitude 95° 11′ W. We had now calms and light breezes succeeding each other till the next morning, when the wind freshened at W.N.W., and was attended with a thick fog and drizzling rain the three following days, during which time we stretched to the north, more to the west; but the strong winds from that direction put it out of my power.

On the 18th the wind veered to south-west, and blew very fresh, but was attended with clear weather, which gave us an opportunity to ascertain our longitude by several lunar observations made by Messrs. Wales, Clerke, Gilbert and Smith. The mean result of all was 94° 19′ 30″ W.; Mr. Kendal's watch, at the same time, gave 94° 46′ W.; our latitude was 43° 53′ S. The wind continued not long at south-west before it veered back to west and west-north-west. As we advanced to the north we felt a most sensible change in the weather. The 20th, at noon, we were in the latitude of 39° 58′ S., longitude 94° 37′ W. The day was clear and pleasant, and I may say the only summer's day we had had since we left New Zealand. The mercury in the thermometer rose to 66.

We still continued to steer to the north, as the wind remained in the old quarter; and the next day, at noon, we were in the latitude 37° 54′ S., which was the same that Juan Fernandez's discovery is said to lie in. We, however, had not the least signs of any land being in our neighborhood. The next day at noon we were in latitude 36° 10′ S., longitude 94° 56′ W. Soon after, the wind veered to south-south-east, and enabled us to steer west-south-west, which I thought the most probable direction to find the land of which we were in search; and yet I had no hopes of succeeding, as we had a large hollow swell from the same point. We, however, continued this course till the 25th, when the wind having veered again round to the westward, I gave it up, and stood away to the north, in order to get to the latitude of Easter Island; our latitude at this time was 37° 52′, longitude 91° 10′ W.

I was now well assured that the discovery of Juan Fernandez, if any such was ever made, can be nothing but a small island; there being hardly room for a large land, as will only appear by the tracks of Captain Wallis, Bougainville, of the Endeavor, and this of the Resolution. Whoever wants to see an account of the discovery in question, will meet with it in Mr. Dalrymple's Collection of Voyages to the South Seas. This gentleman places it under the meridian of 90°, where I think it cannot be; for M. de Bougainville seems to have run down under that meridian, and we had now examined the latitude in which it is said to lie, from the meridian of 94° to 101°. It is not probable it can lie to the east of 90°; because if it did, it must have been seen at one time or other by ships bound from the northern to the southern parts of America. Mr. Pengre, in a little treatise concerning the Transit of Venus, published in 1768, gives some account of land having been discovered by the Spaniards in 1714, in the latitude of 38°, and 550 leagues from the coast of Chili, which is in the longitude of 110° or 111° W., and within a degree or two of my track in the Endeavor; so that this can hardly be its situation. In short, the only probable situation it can have must be about the meridian of 106° or 108° W., and then it can only be a small one, as I have already observed.

I was now taken ill of the bilious colic, which was so violent as to confine me to my bed; so that the management of the ship was left to Mr. Cooper, the first officer, who conducted her very much to my satisfaction. It was several days before the most dangerous symptoms of my disorder were removed; during which time Mr. Patten, the surgeon, was to me not only a skilful physician, but an affectionate nurse; and I should ill deserve the care he bestowed on me if I did not make this public acknowledgment. When I began to recover a favorite dog belonging to Mr. Forster fell a sacrifice to my tender stomach. We had no other fresh meat whatever on board; and I could eat of this flesh, as well as broth made of it, when I could taste nothing else. Thus I received nourishment and strength from that which would have made most people in Europe sick; so true it is, that necessity is governed by no law.

On the 28th, in the latitude of 33° 7′ S., longitude 102° 33′ W. we began to see flying fish, egg-birds, and noddies, which are said not to go above sixty or eighty leagues from land; but of this we have no certainty. No one yet knows to what distance the oceanic birds go to sea; for my own part, I do not believe there is one in the whole tribe that can be relied on, in pointing out the vicinity of land.

In the latitude of 30° 30′ S., longitude 101° 45′ W., we began to see men-of-war birds. In the latitude of 29° 44′, longitude 100° 45′ W., we had a calm for near two days together during which time the heat was intolerable; but what ought to be remarked, was a very great swell from the south-west. On the 6th of March, the calm was succeeded by an easterly wind, with which we steered north-west till noon the 8th, when, being in the latitude of 27° 4′ S., longitude 103° 58′ W., we steered west, meeting every day with great numbers of birds, such as men-of-war, tropic and egg-birds, noddies, sheerwaters &c; and once we passed several pieces of sponge, and a small dried leaf not unlike a bay one. Soon after, we saw a sea-snake, in every respect like those we had before seen at the tropical islands. We also saw plenty of fish; but were such bad fishers, that we caught only four albatross which were very acceptable, to me especially, who was just recovering from my illness.

SEQUEL OF THE PASSAGE FROM NEW ZEALAND TO EASTER ISLAND, TRANSACTIONS THERE, WITH AN ACCOUNT OF AN EXPEDITION TO DISCOVER THE INLAND PART OF THE COUNTRY, AND A DESCRIPTION OF SOME OF THE SURPRISING GIGANTIC STATUES FOUND IN THE ISLAND.

At eight o'clock in the morning on the 11th, land was seen, from the mast-head, bearing west, and at noon from the deck, extending from W. 3/4 N. to W. by S. about twelve league distant. I made no doubt that this was Davis's Land, or Easter Island, as its appearance from this situation corresponded very well with Wafer's account; and we expected to have seen the low sandy isle that Davis fell in with, which would have been a confirmation; in this we were disappointed. At seven o'clock in the evening, the island bore from N.W. to N. 87° W., about five leagues distant; in which situation we sounded, without finding ground, with a line of a hundred and forty fathoms. Here we spent the night, having alternately light airs and calms, till ten o'clock the next morning, when a breeze sprung up at west-south-west. With this we stretched in for the land; and, by the help of the glass, discovered people, and some of those colossian statues or idols mentioned by the authors of Roggeveen's Voyage. At four o'clock in the afternoon, we were half a league south-south-east, and north-north-west of the north-east point of the island; and, on sounding, found thirty-five fathoms, a dark sandy bottom. I now tacked and endeavored to go into what appeared to be a bay, on the west side of the point, or south-east side of the island; but before this could be accomplished, night came upon us, and we stood on and off under the land till the next morning, having soundings from seventy-five to a hundred and ten fathoms, the same bottom as before.

On the 13th, about eight o'clock in the morning, the wind, which had been variable most part of the night, fixed at south-east and blew in squalls, accompanied by rain, but it was not long before the weather became fair. As the wind now blew right on the south-east shore, which does not afford that shelter I at first thought, I resolved to look for anchorage in the west and north-west sides of the island. With this view, I bore up round the south point, off which lie two small islets, the one nearest the point high and peaked, and the other low and flattish. After getting round the point, and coming before a sandy beach, we found soundings, thirty and forty fathoms, sandy ground, and about one mile from the shore. Here a canoe conducted by two men came off to us. They brought with them a bunch of plantains, which they sent into the ship by a rope, and then they returned ashore. This gave us a good opinion of the islanders, and inspired us with hopes of getting some refreshments, which we were in great want of.

I continued to range along the coast till we opened the northern point of the isle without seeing a better anchoring-place than the one we had passed. We therefore tacked, and plied back to it; and, in the mean time, sent away the master in a boat to sound the coast. He returned about five o'clock in the evening, and soon after we came to an anchor, in thirty-six fathoms water, before the sandy beach above mentioned. As the master drew near the shore with the boat, one of the natives swam off to her, and insisted on coming aboard the ship, where he remained two nights and a day. The first thing he did after coming aboard, was to measure the length of the ship, by fathoming her from the taff-rail to the stern; and as he counted the fathoms, we observed that he called the numbers by the same names that they do at Otaheite; nevertheless, his language was in a manner wholly un-intelligible to all of us.

Having anchored too near the edge of the bank, a fresh breeze from the land, about three o'clock the next morning, drove us off it; on which the anchor was heaved up, and sail made to regain the bank again. While the ship was plying in, I went ashore, ac-companied by some of the gentlemen, to see what the island was likely to afford us. We landed at the sandy beach, where some hundreds of the natives were assembled, and who were so im-patient to see us, that many of them swam off to meet the boats. Not one of them had so much as a stick or weapon of any sort in their hands. After distributing a few trinkets amongst them, we made signs for something to eat; on which they brought down a few potatoes, plantains, and sugar-canes, and exchanged them for nails, looking-glasses, and pieces of cloth. We presently dis-covered that they were as expert thieves, and as tricking in their exchanges, as any people we had yet met with. It was with some difficulty we could keep the hats on our heads, but hardly possible to keep anything in our pockets, not even what themselves had sold us; for they would watch every opportunity to snatch it from us, so that we sometimes bought the same thing two or three times over, and after all did not get it.

Before I sailed from England, I was informed that a Spanish ship had visited this isle in 1769. Some signs of it were seen among the people now about us; one man had a pretty good broad-brimmed European hat on, another had a grego jacket, and another a red silk handkerchief. They also seemed to know the use of a musket, and to stand in much awe of it, but this they probably learnt from Roggeveen, who, if we are to believe the authors of that voyage, left them sufficient tokens.

Near the place where we landed were some of those statues before mentioned, which I shall describe in another place. The country appeared barren and without wood; there were, nevertheless, several plantations of potatoes, plantains, and sugar-canes; we also saw some fowls, and found a well of brackish water. As these were articles we were in want of, and as the natives seemed not unwilling to part with them, I resolved to stay a day or two. With this view, I repaired on board, and brought the ship to an anchor in thirty-two fathoms water; the bottom, a fine dark sand. Our station was about a mile from the nearest shore, the south point of a small bay, in the bottom of which is the sandy beach before mentioned, being east south-east distant one mile and a half. The two rocky islets lying off the south point of the island were just shut behind a point to the north of them; they bore half. The two rocky islets lying off the south point of the island bore N. 25° E. distant about six miles. But the best mark for this anchoring-place is the beach; because it is the only one on this side the island. In the afternoon we got on board a few casks of water, and opened a trade with the natives for such things as they had to dispose. Some of the gentlemen also made an excursion into the country to see what it produced and returned again in the evening, with the loss only of a hat, which one of the natives snatched off the head of one of the party.

Early next morning, I sent Lieutenants Pickersgill and Edge-cumbe with a party accompanied by several of the gentlemen, to examine the country. As I was not sufficient recovered from my late illness to make one of the party, I was obliged to content myself remaining at the landing-place among the natives. We had at one time a pretty brisk trade with them for potatoes, which we observed they dug up out of an adjoining plantation; this traffic, which was very advantageous to us, was soon put a stop to by the owner (I supposed) of the plantation coming down, and driving all the people out of it. By this we concluded that he had been robbed of his property, and that they were not less scrupulous of stealing from one another than from us, on whom they practised every little fraud they could think of, and generally with success; for we no sooner detected them in one, they found out another. About seven o'clock in the evening, the party I had sent into the country returned, after having been over the greatest part of the island.

They left the beach about nine o'clock in the morning, and took a path which led to the south-east side of the island, followed by a great crowd of the natives, who preyed much upon them. But they had not proceeded far, before a middle-aged man, punctured from head to foot, and his face painted with a sort of white pigment, appeared with a spear in his hand, and walked alongside of them, making signs to his countrymen to keep a distance, and not to molest our people. When he had pretty well effected this, he hung a piece of white cloth on his spear, placed himself in the front, and led the way with the ensign of peace, as they understood it to be. For the greatest part of the distance across the ground had but a barren appearance, being a dry hard clay, and everywhere covered with stones; but, notwithstanding this, there were several large tracts planted with potatoes, some plantain walks, but they saw no fruit on any of the trees. Towards the highest part of the south end of the island, the soil, which was a fine red earth, seemed much better, with a longer grass, and was not covered with stones as in the other parts; but here they saw neither house nor plantation.

On the east side, near the sea, they met with three platforms of stone-work, or rather the ruins of them. On each had stood four of those large statues; but they were all fallen down from two of them, and also one from the third; all except one were broken by the fall and in some measure defaced. Mr. Wales measured this one, and found it to be fifteen feet in length, and six feet broad over the shoulders. Each statue had on its head a large cylinder stone of a red colour, wrought perfectly round. The one they measured, which was not by far the largest, was fifty-two inches high, and sixty-six in diameter. In some, the upper corner of the cylinder was taken off in a sort of concave quarter-round, but in others the cylinder was entire.

From this place they followed the direction of the coast to the north-east, the man with the flag still leading the way. For about three miles they found the country very barren and in some places stript of the soil to the bare rock, which seemed to be a poor sort of ore. Beyond this they came to the most fertile part of the island they saw, it being interspersed with plantations of potatoes, sugar-canes, and plantain trees, and these not so much encumbered with stones as those which they had seen before; but they could find no water except what the natives twice or thrice brought them, which, though brackish and stinking was rendered acceptable by the extremity of their thirst. They also passed some huts, the owners of which met them with roasted potatoes and sugarcanes, and placing themselves ahead of the foremost of the party, (for they marched in a line in order to have the best of the path,) gave one to each man as he passed by. They observed the same method in distributing the water which they brought; and were particularly careful that the foremost did not drink too much, lest none should be left for the hindmost. But at the very time these were relieving the thirsty and hungry, there were not wanting others who endeavored to steal from them the very things which had been given them. At last, to prevent worse consequences, they were obliged to fire a load of small shot at one who was so audacious as to snatch from one of the men the bag which contained everything they carried with them. The shot hit him on the back; on which he dropped the bag, ran a little way, and then fell; soon afterwards he got up and walked; and what became of him they knew not, nor whether he was much wounded. As this affair occasioned some delay, and drew the natives together, they presently saw the man who had hitherto led the way, and one or two more coming running towards them; but instead of stopping when they came up, they continued to run toward them, repeating in a kind manner, a few words, until our people set forwards again. Soon their old guide hoisted his flag, leading the way as before, and none ever attempted to steal from them the whole day afterwards.

As they passed along, they observed on a hill a number of people collected together, some of whom had spears in their hands; but, on being called to by their countrymen, they dispersed; except a few, amongst whom was one seemingly of some note. He was a stout, well formed man with a fine open countenance; his face was painted, his body punctured, and he had a better Hahou, or cloth, than the rest. He saluted them as he came up, by stretching out his arms with both hands clenched, lifting them over his head, opening them wide, and then letting them fall gradually down to his sides. To this man, whom they understood to be chief of the island, their other friend gave his white flag; and he gave it to another, who carried it before them the remainder of the day.

Towards the eastern end of the island, they met with a well whose water was perfectly fresh, being considerably above the level of the sea; but it was dirty, owing to the filthiness or uncleanness (call it which you will) of the natives, who never go to drink without washing themselves all over as soon as they have done; and if ever so many of them are together, the one leaps right into the middle of the hole, drinks, and washes himself without the least ceremony; after which another takes his place and does the same.

They observed that this side of the island was full of those gigantic statues so often mentioned; some placed in groups on platforms of masonry; others single, fixed only in the soil and that not deep; and these latter are in general much larger than the others. Having measured one which had fallen down, they found it very near twenty-seven feet long, and upwards of eight feet over the breast or shoulders; and yet this appeared considerably short of the size of one they saw standing; its shade, a little past two o'clock, being sufficient to shelter all the party, consisting of near thirty persons, from the rays of the sun. There they stopped to dine; after which they repaired to a hill, from whence they saw all the east and north shores of the island, on which they could not see either bay or creek fit even for a boat to land in, nor the least signs of fresh water. What the natives brought them was real salt water; but they observed that some of them drank pretty plentifully of it; so far will necessity and custom get the better of nature! On this account, they were obliged to return to the last mentioned well; where, after having quenched their thirst, they directed their route across the island towards the ship, as it was now four o'clock.

In a small hollow on the highest part of the island, they met with several such cylinders as are placed on the heads of the statues. Some of these appeared larger than any they had seen before; but it was now too late to stop to measure any of them.

Mr. Wales, from whom I had this information, is of opinion that there had been a quarry here, whence these stones had formerly been dug, and that it would have been no difficult matter to roll them down the hill after they were formed. I think this a very reasonable conjecture, and have no doubt that it has been so. On the declivity of the mountain, towards the west, they met with another well; but the water was a very strong mineral, had a thick green scum on the top, and stunk intolerably. Necessity, however, obliged some to drink of it; but it soon made them so sick, that they threw it up the same way it went down.

In all this excursion, as well as the one made the preceding day, only two or three shrubs were seen. The leaf and seed of one (called by the natives Torromedo) were not much unlike those of the common vetch; but the pod was more like that of a tamarind in its size and shape. The seeds have a disagreeable bitter taste; and the natives, when they saw our people chew them, made signs to spit them out; from whence it was concluded that they think them poisonous. The wood is of a reddish colour, and pretty hard and heavy; but very crooked, small, and short, not exceeding six or seven feet in height. At the south-west corner of the island, they found another small shrub, whose wood was white and brittle in some measure, as also its leaf, resembling the ash. They also saw in several places the Otaheitean cloth plant, but it was poor and weak, and not above two and a half feet at most. They saw not an animal of any sort, and but very few birds; nor indeed anything which can induce ships that are not in the utmost distress to touch at this island.

This account of the excursion I had from Mr. Pickersgill and Mr. Wales, men of whose veracity I could depend; and therefore, I determined to leave the island the next day since nothing was to be obtained that could make it worth my while to stay longer. The water which we had sent on board was not much better than if it had been taken out of the sea. We had a calm until ten o'clock in the morning of the 16th, when a breeze sprang up out of the west, accompanied with heavy showers of rain, which lasted about an hour; the weather then clearing up, we got under sail, stood to sea, and kept plying to and fro; an officer was sent on shore with two boats, to purchase such refreshments as they might have brought down; for I judged this would be the case, as they knew nothing of sailing. The event proved that I was not mistaken; for the boats made two trips that night; when we hoisted them in, and made sail to the north-west with a light north north-east.

A DESCRIPTION OF THE ISLAND, ITS PRODUCE, SITUATION, AND INHABITANTS; THEIR MANNERS AND CUSTOMS—CONJECTURES CONCERNING THEIR GOVERNMENT, RELIGION, AND OTHER SUBJECTS; WITH A MORE PARTICULAR ACCOUNT OF THE GIGANTIC STATUES

I shall now give some further account of this island, which is undoubtedly the same Admiral Roggeveen touched at in April 1722, although the description given of it by the authors of that voyage does by no means agree with it now. It may also be the same one seen by Captain Davis in 1668; for when seen from the east, it answers very well to the description, as I have before observed. In short, if this is not the land, his discovery must lie far from the coast of America, as this latitude had been well explored from the north of 80° to 110°. Captain Carteret carried it much further, but his track seems to have been a litttle too far south. Had I found fresh water, I intended spending some days looking for the low sandy isle Davis fell in with, which would have determined the point; but I did not find water, and had a long run to make before I was assured of getting any, and in want of refreshments, I declined the search, as a small delay might have resulted in bad consequences to the crew, many of them beginning to be more or less affected by the scurvy.

No nation need contend for the honour of the discovery of this island, as there cannot be places which afford less convenience for shipping than it does. Here is no safe anchorage, no wood for fuel, nor any fresh water worth taking on board. Nature has been exceedingly sparing of her favours to this spot. As everything must be raised by dint of labour it cannot be supposed the inhabitants plant much more than is sufficient for themselves and as they are but few in number, they cannot have much to spare to supply the wants of infrequent strangers. The produce in sweet potatoes, yams, taraoreddy-root, plantains, sugar-canes, all pretty good, the potatoes especially, which are the best of the kind in places we visited. Gourds they have also; but so very few, that a cocoa-nut shell was the most valuable thing we could give them. They have a few tame fowls, such as cocks and hens, small but well-tasted. They have also rats, which it seems they eat; for I saw a man with some dead ones in his hand, and he seemed unwilling to part with them, giving me to understand they were for food. Land-birds, there were hardly any, and sea-birds very few; these were men-of-war, tropic, and egg-birds, noddies, tern, &c. The coast seemed not to abound in fish; at least we could catch none with hook and line, and very little we saw amongst the natives.

Such is the produce of Easter Island, or Davis's Land, which is situated in the latitude of 27° 5' S., longitude 109° 46' 20" W. It is about ten or twelve leagues in length with a hilly and stony surface, and an iron-bound shore. The hills are of such a height as to be seen fifteen or sixteen leagues. Off the south end are two rocky islets lying near the shore.

The north and east points of the island rise directly from the sea to a considerable height; between them, on the south-east side, the shore forms an open bay, in which I believe the Dutch anchored. We anchored, as hath been already mentioned, on the west side of the island, three miles to the north of the south point, with the sandy beach bearing east-south-east. This is a very good road with easterly winds, but a dangerous one with westerly, as the other on the south-east side must be with easterly winds.

For this and other bad accommodations already mentioned, nothing but necessity will force any one to touch at this isle, unless it can be done without going much out of the way; in which case touching here may be advantageous, as the people willingly and easily part with such refreshments as they have, and at an easy rate. We certainly received much benefit from the little we got; but few ships can come here without being in want of water, and this want cannot be here supplied. The little we took on board could not be made use of; it being only salt water which had filtrated through a stony beach into a stone.

This the natives had made for the purpose, a little to the southward of the sandy beach so often mentioned, and the water ebbed and flowed into it with the tide.

The inhabitants of this island do not seem to exceed six or seven hundred souls; and the two-thirds of those we saw were males. They either have but few females among them, or else many were restrained from making their appearance during our stay; for though I saw nothing to induce us to believe the men were of a jealous disposition, or the women forbid to appear in public, something of this kind was probably the case. In colour, figures and language, they bear such affinity to the people of the more western isles, that none will doubt that they have had the same origin. It is extraordinary that the same nation should have spread themselves over all the isles in this vast ocean, from New Zealand to this island, which is almost one-fourth part of the circumference of the globe. Many of them have now no other knowledge of each other than what is preserved by antiquated tradition; and they have by length of time become, as it were, different nations, each having adopted some peculiar custom or habit, &c. Nevertheless, a careful observer will soon see the affinity each has to the other.

In general, the people of this isle are a slender race. I did not see a man that would measure six feet; so far are they from being giants, as one of the authors of Roggeveen's voyage asserts. They are brisk and active, have good features, and not disagreeable countenances; are friendly and hospitable to strangers, but as much addicted to pilfering as any of our neighbors. Tattooing, or puncturing the skin, is much used here. The men are marked from head to foot, with figures all nearly alike; only some give them one direction, and some another, as fancy leads. The women are but little punctured; red and white paint an ornament with them, as also with the men; the former is made of turmeric; but what composes the latter I know not. Their clothing is a piece or two of quilted cloth about six feet by four, or a mat. One piece wrapped round their loins, and another over their shoulders, like a complete dress. But the men, for the most part, are in a manner naked, wearing nothing but a slip of cloth betwixt their legs, each end of which is fastened to a cord or belt they wear round the waist. Their cloth is made of the same materials as at Otaheite, viz. the bark of the cloth-plant; but as they have but little of it, our Otaheitean cloth, or indeed any sort of it, came here to a good market.

Their hair, in general, is black; the women wear it long, and sometimes tied up on the crown of the head; but the men wear it and their beard cropped short. Their head-dress is a round fillet adorned with feathers, and a straw bonnet something like a Scotch one; the former, I believe, being chiefly worn by the men, and the latter by the women. Both men and women have very large holes, or rather slits, in their ears, extended to near three inches in length. They sometimes turn this slit over the upper part, and then the ear looks as if the flap was cut off. The chief ear ornaments are the white down of feathers, and rings, which they wear in the inside of the hole, made of some elastic substance, rolled up like a watch-spring. I judged this was to keep the hole at its utmost extension. I do not recall seeing them wear any other ornaments, excepting amulets made of bone or shell; harmless and friendly as these people seem to be, they are not without offensive weapons such as short wooden clubs and spears; which latter are crooked sticks about six feet armed at one end with pieces of flint. They have also a weapon made of wood, the Patoo patoo of New Zealand.

Their houses are low miserable huts, constructed by setting sticks upright in the ground at six or eight feet distance, then bending them towards each other, and tying them together at the top, forming thereby a kind of Gothic arch. The longest sticks are in the middle, and shorter ones each way, and at less distance asunder; by which method the building is highest and broadest in the middle, and lower and narrower towards each side. To these are tied others horizontally, and the whole is thatched over with leaves of cane. The door-way is in the middle of one side, formed like a porch, and so low and narrow as just to admit a man to enter upon all-fours. The largest house I saw was about ten feet long, eight or nine feet high in the middle, and three or four at each end; its breadth in these parts was nearly equal to its height. Some have a kind of vaulted house built of stone, and partly under ground; but I never was in one of these.

I saw no household utensils amongst them except gourds, and of these but very few. They were extravagantly fond of cocoa-nut shells; more so than of anything we could give them. They dress their victuals in the same manner as at Otaheite; that is, with hot stone in an oven or hole in the ground. The straw or tops of sugar-cane, plantain heads, &c. serve for fuel to heat the stones. Plantains, which require but little dressing, they roast in fires of straw, dried grass, &c., and whole races of them are ripened or roasted in this manner. We freqently saw ten or a dozen, or more, such fires in one place, and most common in the mornings and evenings.

No more than three or four canoes were seen on the whole island; and these very narrow and built of many pieces sewed together with small line. They are about eighteen or twenty feet long, head and stern carved or raised a little, are very narrow, and fitted with outriggers. They do not seem capable of carrying above four persons, and are by no means for any distant navigation. As small and as mean as these canoes were, it was a matter of wonder to us where they got the wood to build them with; for in one of them was a board six or eight feet long, fourteen inches broad at one end, and eight at the other; where I did not see a stick on the island which would have made a board half this size; nor, in it was there another piece in the whole canoe half so big.

There are two ways by which it is possible they may have got this large wood; it may have been left there by the Spaniards; or it might have been driven on the shore of the island from some distant land. It is even possible that there may be some land in the neighborhood from whence they might have got it. We, however, saw no signs of any; nor did we get the least information on this head from the natives, although we tried every means we could think of to obtain it. We were almost as unfortunate in our inquiries for the proper or native name of the island. For, on comparing notes, I found we had got three different names for it, viz. Tamareki, Whyhu, and Teapy. Without pretending to know which, or whether any of them is right, I shall only observe, that the last was obtained by Oededee, who understood their language much better than any of us; though even he understood it but very imperfectly.

It appears by the account of Roggeveen's voyage, that these people had no better vessels than when he first visited them. The want of materials, and not of genius, seems to be the reason why they have made no improvement in this art. Some pieces of carving were found amongst them, both well designed and executed. Their plantations are prettily laid out in line, but not inclosed by any fence; indeed, they have nothing for this purpose but stones. I have no doubt that all these plantations are private property and that there are here as at Otaheite, chiefs (which they call Areckes) to whom these plantations belong. But of the power or authority of these chiefs, or of the government of these people, I confess myself quite ignorant.

Nor are we better acquainted with their religion. The gigantic statues so often mentioned are not, in my opinion, looked upon as idols by the present inhabitants, whatever they might have been in the days of the Dutch; at least, I saw nothing that could induce me to think so. On the contrary, I rather suppose that they are burying-places for certain tribes or families. I, as well as some others, saw a human skeleton lying in one of the platforms, covered with stones. Some of these platforms of masonry are thirty or forty feet long, twelve or sixteen broad, and from three to twelve in height; which last in some measure depends on the nature of the ground. For they are generally at the brink of the bank facing the sea, so that this face may be ten or twelve feet or more high, and the other may not be above three or four. They are built, or rather faced, with hewn stones of a very large size; and the workmanship is not inferior to the best plain piece of masonry we have in England. They use no sort of cement; yet the joints are exceedingly close, and the stones morticed and tenanted one into another, in a very artful manner. The side walls are not perpendicular but inclining a little inwards, in the same manner that breast-works, &c., are built in Europe: yet had not all this care, pains, and sagacity been able to preserve these curious structures from the ravages of all devouring time. The statues, or at least many of them, are erected on these platforms, which serve as foundations. They are, as near as we could judge, about half length, ending in a sort of stump at the bottom, on which they stand. The workmanship is rude, but not bad; nor are the features of the face ill formed, the nose and chin in particular; but the ears are long beyond proportion; and, as to the bodies, there is hardly anything like a human figure about them.

I had an opportunity of examining only two or three of these statues, which are near the landing-place; and they were of a grey stone, seemingly of the same sort as that with which the platforms were built. But some of the gentlemen who travelled

over the island, and examined many of them, were of opinion that
the stone of which they were made was different from any other
they saw on the island, and had much the appearance of being
fictitious. We could hardly conceive how these islanders, wholly
unacquainted with any mechanical power, could raise such stupen-
dous figures, and afterwards place the large cylindric stones, upon
their heads. The only method I can conceive, is by raising the
upper end by little and little, supporting it by stones as it is
raised, and building about it till they got it erect; thus a sort of
mount, or scaffolding, would be made, on which they might roll
the cylinder, and place it upon the head of the statue, and then
the stones might be removed from about it. But if the stones
are fictitious, the statues might have been put together on the
place in their present position, and the cylinder put on by building
a mount round them as above mentioned. But, let them have been
made and put up, by this or any other method, they must have
been a work of immense time, and sufficiently show the ingenuity
and perseverance of the islanders in the age in which they were
built; for the present inhabitants have most certainly had no hand
in them, as they do not even repair the foundations of those
which are going to decay. They give different names to them,
such as Gotomoara, Marapate, Kanaro, Gowaytoo-goo, Matta
Matta, &c., to which they sometimes prefix the word Moi, and
sometimes annex Areekee. The latter signifies chief, and the former,
burying, or sleeping-place, as well as we could understand. Besides the monuments of antiquity, which are pretty numerous, and
nowhere right on or near the sea-coast, there were many little
heaps of stones piled up in different places, along the coast. Two
or three of the uppermost stones in each pile were generally
white; perhaps always so, when the pile is complete. It will hardly
be doubted that these piles of stone had a meaning. Probably they
might mark the place where people had been buried, and serve
instead of the large statues.

The working-tools of these people are but very mean, and,
like those of all the other islanders we have visited in this ocean,
made of stone, bone, shells, &c. They set but little value on iron,
or iron tools, which is the more extraordinary as they know their
use; but the reason may be their having but little occasion for
them.

V

LA PEROUSE
SPENDS HALF A DAY

Jean François Galaup de la Pérouse was born at Albi in the ancient Albigensian region of southern France. Since he seems to have been of noble birth he joined the navy as an officer. He distinguished himself by capturing a frigate in the war against England. Popular at court, he proposed a voyage of exploration which would take him around the world.

Louis XVI, who had cultivated an interest in geography, himself drew up the program for the voyage. La Pérouse was given command of two frigates, the *Boussole* and the *Astrolabe*, which were fitted out at Brest for a three-year cruise. They left France in August of 1785.

They rounded the Horn in the summer season and put into the bay of Concepción in southern Chile. There they were received as allies of the Spanish throne and given every facility to refit and revictual. Using Captain Cook's sailing directions and the Spanish charts, they sailed into his old anchorage at Hangaroa.

Things had picked up since Cook's visit. They found the people cheerful and well fed and provisions abundant. During Cook's visit the women must have hidden in caves because he saw very few. The French saw at least three hundred, many children but few old men. They estimated the population at twelve hundred.

Their artists must have worked like beavers. They came away with numerous studies of the ancient architecture and statuary carefully drawn to scale and with numerous sketches which they worked up into engravings to ornament La Pérouse's narrative of his circumnavigation when it came out in Paris. One of the most amusing showed an officer losing the hat he had placed on the pedestal while he admired one of the great statues. A native was inching it away with a crooked stick.

VOYAGE

ROUND THE WORLD,

IN THE YEARS

1785, 1786, 1787, AND 1788.

Description of Easter Island—Occurrences There—
Manners and Customs of the Inhabitants.
(April 1786.)

Cook's Bay, in Easter Island, or Isle de Pâques, is situated in 27° 11′ south latitude, and 111° 55′ west longitude. It is the only anchorage, sheltered from the east and south-east winds, that is to be found in these latitudes; and even here a vessel would run greak risk from westerly winds, but that they never blow from that part of the horizon without previously shifting from east to north-east, to north, and so in succession to the west, which allows time to get under way; and after having stood out a quarter of a league to sea, there is no cause for apprehension. It is easy to know this bay again: after having doubled the two rocks at the south point of the island, it will be necessary to coast along a mile from the shore, till a little sandy creek makes its appearance, which is the most certain mark. When this creek bears east by south, and the two rocks of which I have spoken are shut in by the point, the anchor may be let go in twenty fathoms, sandy bottom, a quarter of a league from the shore. If you have more offing, bottom is found only in thirty-five or forty fathoms, and the depth increases so rapidly that the anchor drags. The landing is easy enough at the foot of one of the statues of which I shall presently speak.

At day-break I made every preparation for our landing. I had reason to flatter myself I should find friends on shore, since I had loaded all those with presents who had come from thence over night; but from the accounts of other navigators, I was well aware, that these Indians are only children of a larger growth, in whose eyes our different commodities appear so desirable as to induce them to put every means in practice to get possession of them. I thought it necessary, therefore, to restrain them by fear, and ordered our landing to be made with a little military parade; accordingly it was effected with four boats and twelve armed soldiers. M. de Langle and myself were followed by all the passengers and officers, except those who were wanted on board to carry on the duty of the two frigates; so that we amounted to about seventy persons, including our boats crews.

Four or five hundred Indians were waiting for us on the shore; they were unarmed; some of them cloathed in pieces of white or yellow stuff, but the greater number naked: many were tatooed, and had their faces painted red; their shouts and countenances were expressive of joy; and they came forward to offer us their hands, and to facilitate our landing.

The island in this part rises about twenty feet from the sea. The hills are seven or eight hundred fathoms inland; and from their base the country slopes with a gentle declivity towards the sea. This space is covered with grass fit for the feeding of cattle; among which are large stones lying loose upon the ground: they appeared to me to be the same as those of the Isle of France, called there *giraumons* (pumpkins), because the greater number are of the size of that fruit: these stones, which we found so troublesome in walking, are of great use, by contributing to the freshness and moisture of the ground, and partly supply the want of the salutary shade of the trees which the inhabitants were so imprudent as to cut down, in times, no doubt, very remote, by which their country lies fully exposed to the rays of the sun, and is destitute of running streams and springs. They were ignorant, that in little islands surrounded by an immense ocean, the coolness of land covered with trees can alone stop and condense the clouds, and thus attract to the mountains abundant rain to form springs and rivulets on all sides. Those islands which are deprived of this advantage are reduced to a dreadful drought, which by degrees destroying the shrubs and plants renders them almost un-inhabitable. M. de Langle and myself had no doubt, that this people owed the misfortune of their situation to the imprudence of their ancestors; and it is probable, that the other islands of the South Sea abound in water, only because they fortunately contain mountains, on which it has been impossible to cut down the woods; thus the liberality of nature to the inhabitants of these latter islands appears, notwithstanding her seeming parsimony in reserving to herself these inaccessible places. A long abode in the Isle of France, which so strikingly resembles Easter Island, has convinced me, that trees never shoot again in such situations, unless they are sheltered from the sea winds, either by other trees or an enclosure of walls; and the knowledge of this fact has discovered to me the cause of the devastation of Easter Island. The inhabitants have much less reason to complain of the eruptions of their volcanoes, long since extinguished, than of their own imprudence. But as man by habit accustoms himself to almost any situation, these people appeared less miserable to me than to captain Cook and Mr. Forster. They arrived here after a long and disagreeable voyage; in want of every thing, and sick of the scurvy; they found neither water, wood, nor hogs; a few fowls, bananas, and potatoes are but feeble resources in these circumstances. Their narratives bear testimony to their situation. Ours was infinitely better: the crews enjoyed the most perfect health; we had taken in at Chili every thing that was necessary for many months, and we only desired of these people the privilege of doing them good: we brought them goats, sheep, and hogs; we had seeds of orange, lemon, and cotton trees, of maize, and, in short, of every species of plants, which was likely to flourish in the island.

Our first care after landing was to form an enclosure with armed soldiers ranged in a circle; and having enjoined the inhabitants to leave this space void, we pitched a tent in it; I then ordered to be brought on shore the various presents that I intended for them, as well as the different animals: but as I had expressly forbidden the men to fire, or even keep at a distance, by the butt ends of their firelocks, such of the Indians as might be too troublesome, the soldiers soon found themselves exposed to the rapacity of the continually increasing numbers of these islanders. They were at least eight hundred; and in this number there were certainly a hundred and fifty women. The faces of these were many of them agreeable; and they offered their favours to all those who would make them a present. The Indians would engage us to accept them, by themselves setting the example. They were only separated from the view of the spectators by a simple covering of the stuff of the country, and while our attention was attracted by the women, we were robbed of our hats and handkerchiefs. They all appeared to be accomplices in the robbery; for scarcely was it accomplished, than like a flock of birds they all fled at the same instant; but seeing that we did not make use of our firelocks, they returned a few minutes after, recommended their caresses, and watched the moment for committing a new depredation: this proceeding continued the whole morning. As we were obliged to go away at night, and had so little time to employ in their education, we determined to amuse ourselves with the tricks made use of to rob us; and at length, to obviate every pretence that might lead to dangerous consequences, I ordered them to restore to the soldiers and sailors the hats which had been taken away. The Indians were unarmed; three or four only, out of the whole number, had a kind of wooden club, which was far from being formidable. Some of them seemed to have a slight authority over the others: I took them for chiefs, and distributed medals among them, which I hung around their necks by a chain, but I soon found that these were the most notorious thieves; and although they had the appearance of pursuing those who took away our handkerchiefs, it was easy to perceive that they did so with the most decided intention not to overtake them.

Having only eight or ten hours to remain upon the island, and wishing to make the most of our time, I left the care of the tent and all our effects to M. D'Escures, my first lieutenant, giving him charge besides of all the soldiers and sailors who were on shore. We then divided ourselves into two parties; the first, under the command of M. de Langle, was to penetrate as far as possible into the interior of the island, to sow seeds in all such places as might appear favorable to vegetation, to examine the soil, plants, cultivation, population, monuments, and in short everything which might be interesting among this very extraordinary people: those who felt themselves strong enough to take a long journey, accompanied him; among these were Messieurs Dagelet, de Lamanon, Duche, Dufresne, de la Martinière, father Recéveur, the Abbé Monges, and the gardener. The second, of which I was one, contented itself with visiting the monuments, terraces, houses, and plantations within the distance of a league round our establishment. The drawing of these monuments made by Mr. Hodges was a very imperfect representation of what we saw. Mr. Forster thinks that they are the work of a people much more considerable than is at present found here; but his opinion appears to me by no means well founded. The largest of the rude busts which are upon these terraces, and which we measured, is only fourteen feet six inches in height, seven feet six inches in breadth across the shoulders, three feet in thickness round the belly, six feet broad, and five feet thick at the base; these might well be the work of the present race of inhabitants, whose numbers I believe, without the smallest exaggeration, amount to two thousand. The number of women appeared to be nearly that of the men, and the children seemed to be in the same proportion as in other countries; and although out of about twelve hundred persons, who on our arrival collected in the neighborhood of the bay, there were at most three hundred women, I have not drawn any other conjecture from it, than that the people from the extremity of the island had come to see our ships, and that the women, either from greater delicacy, or from being more employed in the management of their family affairs and children, had remained in their houses; consequently that we saw only those who inhabit the vicinity of the bay. The narrative of M. de Langle confirms this opinion; he met in the interior of the island a great many women and children; and we all entered into those caverns in which Mr. Forster and some officers of captain Cook thought at first that the women might be concealed. These are subterraneous habitations, of the same form as those which I shall presently describe, and in which we found little faggots, the largest piece of which was not five feet in length, and did not exceed six inches in diameter. It is however certain, that the inhabitants hid their women when captain Cook visited them in 1772; but it is impossible for me to guess the reason of it, and we are indebted, perhaps, to the generous manner in which he conducted himself towards these people, for the confidence they put in us, which has enabled us to form a more accurate judgment of their population.

All the monuments which are at this time in existence, and of which M. Duche has given a very exact drawing, appeared to be very ancient; they are situated in morais (or burying places) as far as we can judge from the great quantity of bones which we found hard by. There can be no doubt that the form of their present government may have so far equalized their condition, that there no longer exists among them a chief of sufficient authority to employ a number of men in erecting a statue to perpetuate his memory. These colossal images are at present superseded by small pyramidal heaps of stones, the topmost of which is whitewashed. These species of mausoleums, which are only the work of an hour for a single man, are piled up upon the sea shore; and one of the natives shewed us that these stones covered a tomb, by laying himself down at full length on the ground; afterwards, raising his hands towards the sky, he appeared evidently desirous of expressing that they believed in a future state. I was upon my guard against this opinion but having seen this sign repeated by many, and M. de Langle, who had penetrated into the interior of the island, having reported the same fact, I no longer entertained a doubt of it, and I believe that all our officers and passengers partook in this opinion; we did not however perceive traces of any worship, for I do not think that any one can take the statues for idols, although these Indians may have shewed a kind of veneration for them. These busts of colossal size, the dimensions of which I have already given, and which strongly prove the small progress they have made in sculpture, are formed of a volcanic production known to naturalists by the name of Lapillo: this is so soft and light a stone, that some of captain Cook's officers thought it was artificial, composed of a kind of mortar which had been hardened in the air. No more remains, but to explain how it was possible to raise, without engines, so very considerable a weight; but as it is certainly a very light volcanic stone, it would be easy, with levers five or six fathoms long, and by slipping stones underneath, as captain Cook very well explains it, to lift a much more considerable weight; a hundred men would be sufficient for this purpose, for indeed there would not have been room for more.

Thus the wonder disappears; we restore to nature her stone of Lapillo, which is not factitious; and have reason to think, that if there are no monuments of modern construction in the island, it is because all ranks in it are become equal, and that a man has but little temptation to make himself king of a people almost naked, and who live on potatoes and yams; and on the other hand, these Indians not being able to go to war from the want of neighbors, have no need of a chief.

I can only hazard conjectures upon the manners of this people, whose language I did not understand, and whom I saw only during the course of one day; but possessing the experience of former navigators, from an acquaintance with their narratives, I was able to add to them my own observations.

Scarcely a tenth part of the land in this island is under cultivation; and I am persuaded that three days labour of each Indian is sufficient to procure their annual subsistence. The ease with which the necessaries of life are provided induced me to think, that the productions of the earth were in common. Besides, I am nearly certain the houses are common, at least to a whole village or district. I measured one of those houses near our tent; it was three hundred and ten feet in length, ten feet broad, and ten feet high in the middle; its form was that of a canoe reversed: the only entrances were by two doors, two feet high, through which it was necessary to creep on hands and feet. This house is capable of containing more than two hundred persons: it is not the dwelling of any chief, for there is not any furniture in it, and so great a space would be useless to him; it forms a village of itself, with two or three small houses at a little distance from it. There is, probably, in every district a chief, who superintends the plantations. Captain Cook thought that this chief was the proprietor of it; but if this celebrated navigator found some difficulty in procuring a considerable quantity of yams and potatoes, it ought rather to be attributed to the scarcity of these eatables, than to the necessity of obtaining an almost general consent to their being sold.

As for the women, I dare not decide whether they are common to a whole district, and the children to the republic: certain it is that no Indian appeared to have the authority of a husband over any one of the women, and if they are private property, it is a kind of which the possessors are very liberal.

I have already mentioned, that some of the houses are sub-terraneous; but others are built with reeds, which proves that there are marshy places in the interior of the island. The reeds are very skilfully arranged, and are a sufficient defence against the rain. The building is supported by pillars of cut stone, eighteen inches thick; in these, holes are bored at equal distances, through which pass long poles, which form an arched frame; the space between is filled up with reed thatch.

There can be no doubt, as captain Cook observes, of the identity of this people with that of the other islands of the South Sea: they have the same language, and the same cast of features: their cloth is also made of the bark of the mulberry tree; but this is very scarce, on account of the drought, which has destroyed those trees. The few remaining are only three feet high; and even these are obliged to be surrounded with fences to keep off the wind, for the trees never exceed the height of the wall by which they are sheltered.

I have no doubt, that formerly these people enjoyed the same productions as those of the Society Islands. The fruit trees must have perished from the drought, as well as the dogs and hogs, to whom water is absolutely necessary. But man, who in Hudson's Streights drinks the oil of the whale, accustoms himself to every thing, and I have seen the natives of Easter Island drink the sea water like the albatrosses at Cape Horn. We were there in the rainy season, and a little brackish water was found in some holes on the sea shore; they offered it to us in their calabashes, but it disgusted even those who were most thirsty. I do not expect, that the hogs which I have given them will multiply; but I have great hopes, that the sheep and goats, which drink but little, and are fond of salt, will prosper among them.

At one o'clock in the afternoon I returned to the tent, with the intention of going on board, in order that M. de Clonard, the next in command, might, in his turn, come on shore: I there found almost every one without either hat or handkerchief; our forbearance had emboldened the thieves, and I had fared no better than the rest. An Indian who had assisted me to get down from a terrace, after having rendered me this service, took away my hat, and fled at full speed, followed as usual by the rest. I did not order him to be pursued, not being willing to have the exclusive right of being protected from the fun, and observing that almost every person was without a hat, I continued to examine the terrace, a monument that has given me the highest opinion of the abilities of the earlier inhabitants for building, for the pompous word architecture cannot with propriety be made use of here. It appears that they have never had the least knowledge of any cement, but they cut and divide the stones in the most perfect manner; they were also placed and joined together according to all the rules of art.

I made a collection of specimens of these stones; they consist of lava of different compactness. The lightest, and that which consequently would be the soonest decomposed, forms the outer foil in the interior of the island; that which is next the sea consists of a lava much more compact, so as to make a longer resistance; but I do not know any instrument or matter hard enough, in the possession of these islanders, to cut the latter stones; perhaps a longer continuance on the island might have furnished me with some explanations on this subject. At two o'clock I returned on board and M. de Clonard went on shore. Soon afterwards two officers of the *Astrolabe* arrived, to inform me that the Indians had just committed a new theft, which might be attended with more serious consequences. Some divers had cut under water the small cable of the *Astrolabe*'s boat, and had taken away her grapnel, which had not been discovered till the robbers were pretty far advanced into the interior of the island. As this grapnel was necessary to us, two officers and several soldiers pursued them; but they were assailed by a shower of stones. A musket, loaded with powder and fired in the air, had no effect; they were at length under the necessity of firing one with small shot, some grains of which doubtless struck one of those Indians, for the stoning ceased, and our officers were able peaceably to regain our tent; but it was impossible to overtake the robbers, who must have been astonished at not having been able to weary our patience.

They soon returned around our tent, recommenced the offers of their women, and we were as good friends as at our first interview. At length, at six in the evening, every thing was re-embarked, the boats had returned on board, and I made the signal to prepare for sailing. Before we got under way, M. de Langle gave me an account of his journey into the interior of the island, which

I shall relate in the following chapter: he had sown the seeds in different parts of the road, and had given the islanders proofs of the greatest good will towards them. I will, however, finish their portrait by relating, that a sort of chief, to whom M. de Langle made a present of a he and she goat, received them with one hand, and robbed him of his handkerchief with the other.

It is certain, that these people have not the same ideas of theft that we have; with them, probably no shame is attached to it; but they very well knew, that they committed an unjust action, since they immediately took to flight, in order to avoid the punishment which they doubtless feared, and which we should certainly have inflicted on them in proportion to the crime, had we made any considerable stay in the island; for our extreme lenity might have ended by producing disagreeable consequences.

No one, after having read the narratives of the later navigators, can take the Indians of the South Sea for savages; they have on the contrary made very great progress in civilization, and I think them as corrupt as the circumstances in which they are placed will allow them to be. This opinion of them is not founded upon the different thefts which they committed, but upon the manner in which they effected them. The most hardened rogues of Europe are not such great hypocrites as these islanders; all their caresses were feigned; their countenances never expressed a single sentiment of truth; and the man of whom it was necessary to be most distrustful, was the Indian to whom a present had that moment been made, and who appeared the most eager to return for it a thousand little services.

They brought to us by force young girls of thirteen or fourteen years of age, in the hope of receiving pay for them; the repugnance of those young females was a proof, that in this respect the custom of the country was violated. Not a single Frenchman made use of the barbarous right which was given him; and if there were some moments dedicated to nature, the desire and consent were mutual, and the women made the first advances.

I found again in this country all the arts of the Society Isles, but with much fewer means of exercising them, for want of the raw materials. Their canoes have also the same form, but they are composed only of very narrow planks, four or five feet long, and at most can carry but four men. I have only seen three of them in this part of the island, and I should not be much surprised, if in a short time, for want of wood, there should not be a single one remaining here. They have besides learned to make shift without them; and they swim so expertly, that in the most tempestuous sea they go two leagues from the shore, and in returning to land, often, by way of frolic, choose those places where the surf breaks with the greatest fury.

The coast appeared to me not to abound much in fish, and I believe that the inhabitants live chiefly on vegetables; their food consists of potatoes, yams, bananas, sugar canes, and a small fruit which grows upon the rocks on the sea-shore, similar to the grapes that are found in parts adjacent to the tropic in the Atlantic Ocean; the few fowls that are found upon the island cannot be considered as a resource. Our navigators did not meet with any land bird, and even sea fowl are not very common.

The fields are cultivated with a great deal of skill. They root up the grass, lay it in heaps, burn it, and thus fertilize the earth with its ashes. The banana trees are planted in a straight line. They also cultivate the garden nightshade, but I am ignorant what use they make of it; if I knew they had vessels which could stand fire, I should think, that, as at Madagascar or the Isle of France, they eat it in the same manner as they do spinage; but they have no other method of cooking their provision than that of the Society Isles, which consists in digging a hole, and covering their yams and potatoes with red hot stones and embers, mixed with earth, for that every thing which they eat is cooked as in an oven.

The exactness with which they measured the ship showed, that they had not been inattentive spectators of our arts; they examined our cables, anchors, compass, and wheel, and they returned the next day with a cord to take the measure over again, which made me think, that they had had some discussions on shore upon the subject, and that they had still doubts relative to it. I esteem them far less, because they appeared to me capable of reflection. One reflection will, perhaps, escape them, namely, that we employed no violence against them; though they were not ignorant of our being armed, since the mere presenting a firelock in sport made them run away: on the contrary, we landed on the island only with an intention to do them service; we heaped presents upon them, we caressed the children; we sowed in their fields all kinds of useful seeds; presented them with hogs, goats, and sheep, which probably will multiply; we demanded nothing in return: nevertheless they threw stones at us, and robbed us of every thing which it was possible for them to take away. It would, perhaps, have been imprudent in other circumstances to conduct ourselves with so much lenity; but I had resolved to go away in the evening, and I flattered myself that at day-break, when they no longer perceived our ships, they would attribute our speedy departure to the just displeasure we entertained at their proceedings, and that this reflection might amend them; though this idea is a little chimerical, it is of no great consequence to navigators, as the island offers scarcely any resource to ships that may touch there, besides being at no great distance from the Society Isles.

JOURNEY OF M. DE LANGLE
INTO THE INTERIOR OF EASTER ISLAND—
NEW OBSERVATIONS UPON THE MANNERS
AND THE ARTS OF THE NATIVES,
UPON THE QUALITY
AND CULTIVATION OF THE SOIL, &C.
(APRIL 1786)

"I set out at eight o'clock in the morning, accompanied by Messrs. Dagelet, de Lamanon, Dufresne, Duche, the abbé Monges, Father Recéveur, and the gardener; we bent our course from the shore two leagues to the eastward, towards the interior of the island; the walk was very painful, across hills covered with volcanic stones; but I soon perceived that there were foot paths, by which we might easily proceed from house to house; we availed ourselves of these, and visited many plantations of yams and potatoes. The soil of these plantations consisted of a very fertile vegetable earth, which the gardener judged proper for the cultivation of our seeds: he sowed cabbages, carrots, beets, maize and pumpkins; and we endeavored to make the islanders understand, that these seeds would produce roots and fruits which they might eat. They perfectly comprehended us, and from that moment pointed out to us the best spots, signifying to us the places in which they were desirous of seeing our new productions. We added to the leguminous plants, seeds of the orange, lemon, and cotton trees, making them comprehend, that these were trees, and that what we had before sown were plants.

"We did not meet with any other small shrubs than the paper mulberry tree, and the mimosa. There were also pretty considerable fields of garden nightshade, which these people appeared to me to cultivate in the lands already exhausted by yams and potatoes. We continued our route towards the mountains, which, though of considerable height, are all easy of access, and covered with grass; we perceived no marks of any torrent or ravine. After having gone about two leagues to the east, we returned southward towards the shore which we had coasted the evening before, and upon which, by the assistance of our telescopes, we had perceived a great many monuments; several were overthrown, it appeared that these people did not employ themselves in repairing them; others were standing upright, their bases half destroyed. The largest of those that I measured was sixteen feet ten inches in height, including the capital, which was three feet one inch, and which is of a porous lava, very light; its breadth over the shoulders was six feet seven inches, and its thickness at the base two feet seven inches.

"Having perceived a small village, I directed my course towards it; one of the houses was three hundred feet in length, and in the form of a canoe reversed. Very near this place we observed the foundations of several others, which no longer existed; they are composed of stones of cut lava, in which are holes about two inches across. This part of the island appeared to us to be in a much better state of cultivation, and more populous, than the parts adjacent to Cook's Bay. The monuments and terraces were also in greater number. We perceived upon some of the stones, of which those terraces are composed, some rude sculptures of skeletons; and we also saw there holes which were stopped up with stones, by which we imagined, that they might form a communication with the caverns containing the bodies of the dead. An Indian explained to us, by very expressive signs, that they deposited them there, and that afterwards they ascended to heaven. We found upon the sea-shore pyramids of stones, ranged very nearly in the same form as cannon balls in a park of artillery, and we perceived some human bones in the vicinity of those pyramids, and of those statues, all of which had the back turned towards the sea. In the morning we visited seven different terraces, upon which there were statues, some upright, others thrown down, differing from each other only in size; the injuries of time were more or less apparent on them, according to their antiquity. We found near the farthest a kind of mannikin of reed, representing a human figure, ten feet in height; it was covered with a white stuff of the country, the head of a natural size, but the body slender, the limbs in nearly exact proportion; from its neck hung a net, in the shape of a basket, covered with white stuff, which appeared to be filled with grass. By the side of this bag was the image of a child, two feet in length, the arms of which were placed across, and the legs pendant. This mannikin could not have existed many years; perhaps it was a model of some statues to be erected in honour of the chiefs of the country. Near this same terrace there were two parapets, which formed an enclosure of three hundred and eighty-four feet in length, by three hundred and twenty-four in breadth: we were not able to ascertain whether it was a reservoir for water, or the beginning of a fortress; but it appeared to us, that this work had never been finished.

"Continuing to bend our course to the west, we met about twenty children, who were walking under the care of some women, and who appeared to go towards the houses of which I have already spoken.

"At the south end of the island we saw the crater of an old volcano, the size, depth, and regularity of which excited our admiration; it is in the shape of a truncated cone; its superior base, which is the largest, appeared to be more than two thirds of a league in circumference: the lower base may be estimated, by supposing that the side of the cone makes with the axis an angle of about 30°. This lower base forms a perfect circle; the bottom is marshy, containing large pools of fresh water, the surface of which appeared to be above the level of the sea; the depth of this crater is at least eight hundred feet.

"Father Recéveur, who descended into it, related to us, that this marsh was surrounded by some beautiful plantations of banana and mulberry trees. It appears, according to our observations in sailing along the coast, that a considerable portion of it has rolled down on the side next the sea, thus occasioning a great breach in the crater; the height of this breach is one third of the whole cone, and its breadth a tenth of the upper circumference. The grass which has sprung up on the sides of the cone, the swamps which are at the bottom, and the fertility of the adjacent lands, are proofs that the subterraneous fires have a long time been extinct. The only birds which we met with in the island we saw at the bottom of the crater; these were terns. Night obliged me to return towards the ships. We perceived near a house a great number of children, who ran away at our approach: it appeared to us probable, that this house was the habitation of all the children of the district. There was too little difference in their ages for them all to belong to the two women who seemed to be charged with the care of them. There was near this house a hole in the earth, in which they cooked yams and potatoes, according to the manner practiced in the Society Isles.

"On our return to the tent, I presented to three of the natives the three different species of animals which we had destined for them.

"These islanders are hospitable; they several times presented us with potatoes and sugar canes; but they never let an opportunity slip of robbing us, when they could do it with impunity. Scarcely a tenth part of the island is cultivated; the lands which are cleared are in the form of a regular oblong, and without any kind of enclosure: the remainder of the island, even to the summit of the mountains, is covered with a coarse grass. It was the rainy season when we were there, and we found the earth moistened at least a foot deep; some holes in the hills contained a little fresh water, but we did not find in any part the least appearance of a stream. The land seemed to be of a good quality, and there would be a far more abundant vegetation if it were watered. We did not obtain from these people the knowledge of any instrument, which they used for the cultivation of their fields. Probably, after having cleared them, they dig holes in them with wooden stakes, and in this manner plant their yams and potatoes. We very rarely met with a few bushes of mimosa, whose largest branches are only three inches in diameter. The most probable conjectures that can be formed as to the government of these people are, that they consist only of a single nation, divided into as many districts as there are morais, because it is to be observed, that the villages are built near those burying places. The products of the earth seem to be common to all the inhabitants of the same district; and as the men, without any regard to delicacy, make offers of the women to strangers, it is natural to suppose, that they do not belong to any man in particular; and that when the children are weaned, they are delivered over to the management of other women, who, in every district, are charged with the care of bringing them up.

"Twice as many men are met with as women, and if indeed the latter are not less numerous, it is because they keep more at home than the men. The whole population may be estimated at two thousand people; several houses that we saw building, and a great number of children, ought to induce a belief that it does not diminish; there is however reason to think, that the population was more considerable when the island was better wooded. If these islanders had industry enough to build cisterns, they would thereby remedy one of the greatest misfortunes of their situation, and perhaps they would prolong their lives. There is not a single man seen in this island who appears to be above the age of sixty-five, if we can form any estimate of the age of people with whom we are so little acquainted, and whose manner of life differs so essentially from our own."

VI

YOUNG PIERRE LOTI'S ACCOUNT

Pierre Loti—it was a nom de plume—was born Louis Marie Julien Viaud in the old French seafaring town of Rochefort. Since he came of a family of naval officers it was natural that he should go to sea as a midshipman. He was still a very young man when a training cruise on the warship *La Flore* gave him an opportunity to spend several days on Easter Island. He earned his way ashore by making sketches of the archaeological ruins for the admiral and the ship's officers. His account of the island, which went for many years unpublished, was one of his first efforts to establish the remarkably evocative style which later brought him fame with *Pêcheur d'Islande* and *Mme. Chrysanthème*. One of his watercolors he dedicated to the young Sarah Bernhardt. He was awarded the ribbon of the Legion of Honor and was elected to the Académie Française, over Emile Zola by the way, in 1891. After twenty-five years' service he resigned from the navy. He lived on late into the twentieth century.

YOUNG PIERRE LOTI'S ACCOUNT

There exists in the midst of the great ocean, in a region where nobody goes, a mysterious and isolated island; no other land is

*near it and for more than eight hundred leagues in all directions
empty and terrifying immensities surround it.*

*The island is planted with monstrous great statues, the work of
I don't know what race, today degenerate or vanished; its past
remains an enigma.*

*I went ashore there years ago in my green youth from a sailing
frigate, after days of strong wind and obscuring clouds; there
has remained with me the recollection of a half fantastic land, a
land of dreams.*

*In my midshipman's notebook I noted my impressions day by
day amid a lot of childishness and incoherence.*

*It is this child's journal which I am now trying to disentangle,
in an effort to give it the precision it needs.*

January 3, 1872

At eight in the morning the lookout calls land ho and the
silhouette of Easter Island appears dimly in the northwest. The
distance is still great, and it will be evening before we get there
in spite of our speed on the wings of the trade wind.

Several days back we left, to arrive here, the common shiplanes
across the Pacific, for Easter Island lies in no one's path. Discovered by chance the rare navigators who have from time to
time visited the island have brought back contradictory reports.
The populations whose origins are veiled in mystery is becoming
extinct for reasons that we don't know. There remain only several
dozen savages starving and fearful who live on roots, soon to be
reduced to complete solitude, of which the giant statues will be
the only guardians. There is nothing to be found there, not a spring
where you can make provision of fresh water and the reefs and
breakers often make it impossible to land.

We are going ashore to explore the island and to take off if
possible one of the ancient statues which our admiral wants to
carry back to France.

Slowly the land approaches. Outlines sharpen. It lifts up its
red craters and gloomy rocks under a dark cloudy sky. A gust
of wind covers the sea with foam.

Rapa Nui is the name the natives give to Easter Island and in the mere sound of the word I find vibrations of savagery and night; these heavy clouds with which the land veils itself are what my imagination had expected.

Finally at four in the afternoon in the shelter of the island in Cook's Bay where he anchored years ago our frigate furls her sails and lets go her anchors. Several canoes pull out from this strange coast and advance in our direction in the gusty wind.

Here's even a sort of whale boat which is bringing out what seems to be a European. A character in hat and overcoat is coming on board from Rapa Nui. That sends my preconceived notions helter skelter. I feel disenchanted. The visitor comes aboard. It is an elderly Dane, a most unexpected visitor.

His story is that three years ago he had a Tahitian schooner, taking mother-of-pearl and pearls to the American coast make a detour of two hundred leagues to land him here. Since then he lives alone with the natives, an old adventurer as separate from our world as if he had fixed his residence on the moon. An American planter had furnished him with sweet potatoes and yams with the idea of preparing immense future plantations, but nothing grew. The natives flatly refused to work. Two or three hundred of them are grouped around the bay where we anchored. The rest of the island had become a wilderness. The Dane lived in a stone house. He had fixed the roof. The French missionaries had lived there some time back—because there were during several seasons, missionaries at Rapa Nui—but they had gone away or died none seemed to know, leaving the population to relapse to fetishism and idolatry.

While he is talking to us I hear something light give a bound behind me, and I turn to look. One of the Dane's rowers has had the nerve to climb aboard. What an extraordinary lean figure with a small falcon's face and the eyes too close together, too large too sad and wandering. He is naked, at the same time very lean and heavily muscled. His skin of a reddish copper color, is ornamented with blue tattooing; his hair is of an artificial red bound up with scabiosa stems to the top of his head forming a red pompadour which the wind stirs like a flame. He looks at us with all the amazement of eyes too wide open. In every move there is a sort of impish charm.

And the statues? we ask the Danish Crusoe.

Oh the statues. There are two types, those along the beaches that have all been overturned and broken. We'll find some near the environs of the bay. Then there are the others, the frightening ones, from a different age or period. These are still standing way off over there on the other side of the island where no one goes any more. He's getting tamer, the savage with the red topknot. To please us he is dancing and singing. He is one of those that the missionaries baptized. His name is Petro. The wind, increasing with dusk carries off his melancholy song and tosses his topknot about.

But the others are afraid and don't want to come aboard. Their canoes surround the ship more and more shaken by the waves, buried under foam and backwash. Pointing at their naked limbs they demand by signs some exchange from the sailors for their paddles and their lances and their idols of wood and stone that they have brought to trade. The whole population has rushed out naively overexcited by our presence. The sea in the bay is getting savage. Night falls.

4th January

Five in the morning, dawn is breaking under heavy grey clouds. A whale boat which was confided to me carries me ashore with two other midshipmen, my comrades as much in a hurry as I am to set foot on the strange island. The admiral, amused by our impatience, has thought up different commissions for each one; to find the best landing place, to search out the great statues,—and for his breakfast to kill some rabbits.

The sky is cold and gloomy. The wind is in our faces. The trade wind throws salt spume in our faces. The island has put on its most fantastic appearance to receive us. Against the dark grays of the sky the rocks and craters seem a pale copper color. Not a tree anywhere: desert, desolation.

Without too much difficulty we find a passage through the surf which this morning makes a great threatening racket. Once past the fringe of reefs, reaching calm water, free from wind we see Petro our friend from last night, who calls to us from his perch on a rock. His cries wake up the whole population and in an instant the beach is covered with savages. They come out of every hole from the cracks in the rock where they sleep, from huts so low they seem too small to harbor human beings. In the distance we had not noticed the straw huts; they are quite numerous, strangely flattened to the soil. They carry its color.

We had hardly disembarked at the spot Petro pointed out before we were hemmed in by the men of the village. They shake in our faces in the early morning dusk their lances pointed with obsidian and their paddles and their old idols. The wind redoubles its force, lashing and cold. The clouds seem to drag on the ground.

The whale boat that brought us ashore returns to the frigate according to the commandant's orders. My two comrades who have the shotguns go off along the beach towards the rabbit territory which the Dane pointed out the night before and I am left alone crowded between my new hosts, faces and chests blue with tattooing, long hair, strange smiles from their white teeth and mournful eyes of which the whites look whiter than ever on account of the designs in dark blue that surround them. I'm shaking with cold under my light clothing damp from the sea's wetting and I find full daylight slow in coming this morning under such a thick cloud cover. They have me closed in on all sides each one presenting his lance or his idol, now they are singing first humming but then singing a plaintive lugubrious chorus accompanied by a balancing of the head and legs as if they were enormous bears. . . . I know that they are inoffensive. Their faces under the tattooing that gives them such a fierce look really wear expressions of a childish sweetness; they inspire me with no reasonable fear; but all the same penetrating for the first time an island of the great ocean a shiver of surprise and instinctive fright comes over me at feeling all these eyes and these breaths before daylight on a desolate shore in such black weather.

The rhythm of the song speeds up, the movement of heads and thighs becomes faster and faster, voices become hoarse and deep as the song in the wind and the sound of the sea rises to a savage clamor to the rhythm of a furious dance.

Then brusquely they become quiet. The circle opens and the dancers disperse. . . . What did they want, all of them? Some childishness on their part or conjunction or welcoming good wishes. Who can know?

An old tattooed man, wearing long black feathers stuck on his head, undoubtedly some chief, takes me by one hand; Petro takes me by the other and they run with me, the whole crowd following. They stop before one of the reed houses, flattened between the rocks and the sand like the backs of sleeping beasts.

They invite me in. I have to do this on all fours like a cat going through a cat door, since the entrance, level with the earth and guarded by two divinities of evil aspect, is a round hole hardly two feet high.

Inside it's impossible to see a thing on account of the crowd pressing all around; there is no way of standing up, especially after the vivifying air out of doors it is hard to breathe. The place smells like a tannery.

I am invited to sit down on some mats beside the chieftainess and her daughter. I am made to understand that they have no gift to offer me. They are excusing themselves in dumb show. Now that my eyes are accustomed to the light I can see that the place swarms with cats and rabbits.

During the morning I am forced to make many visits of the same sort, to please the notables of the island and I crawl into I hardly know how many obscure dwellings. The crowd follows after closing me in with a confusion of chests and thighs, naked and tattooed. I am drenched with a smell of the wild and savage.

All of them want to give me idols or clubs and lances in exchange for pieces of clothing or objects that amuse them. Money naturally means nothing to them, only good for ornaments on collars, but glass beads have a finer effect. Outdoors the aspect of things changes; the curtain of clouds is tearing to pieces. With more light the island seems more real, less sinister. I'm getting used to it. Already for trading I have given up everything I had in my pockets, my handkerchief, my matches, a notebook and a pencil: I am resolved to give up my midshipman's vest in exchange for an extraordinary war club that ends in a sort of Janus with two human faces. . . . I continue my stroll in shirtsleeves.

Decidedly I've fallen in with a people of children. Young and old never seem to tire of looking at me, listening to me, following me and carrying behind me my diverse acquisition, my idols and my arms singing always the same plaintive melodies. When you think of it our presence on this isolated island must be a considerable event. The immensities of ocean hardly bring them a sail once in ten years.

Outside of the procession that keeps its distance, I have made my little friendships. There are five. Petro first, then two young boys, Atamou and Houga and two girls, Marie and Iouaritai. They are both naked except for a belt that drops down a little in the essential places. They would be quite white without the tan from the sun and the sea which gives them that light coppery tan which seems the mark of the race. Long blue tattoo marks, in bizarre and delightful designs run down their flanks to accentuate the sveltness of their figures. Marie who as a child was baptized by the missionaries—that name of Marie applied to a girl from Easter Island throws you off a little—can only boast of her stance of a young goddess, her freshness and her teeth but Iouaritai would pass for beautiful in any country on earth, with her fine little nose and her great timid eyes. She has knotted her hair in ancient Greek style. It has been dyed a reddish tone and she has ornamented it with flowering grass.

Good god how time passes. It is already half past ten, time for us to go back aboard ship for our breakfast. I can see the whale boat jumping the lines of reef, the whale boat which is to pick us up. My comrades are returning from the hunt followed as I was by a singing procession. They have killed several white sea gulls which they distribute to the women, but not a rabbit. All three of us are pretty poor fellows to entrust with commissions. And the big statues I was going to look for. I must admit that I forgot all about them.

On board we were quite well received, all the same; the officers were interested in all the things we brought back. I was restless and by noon I was on my way back to shore to see my savage friends.

Arriving at the shore I can see that for the island it is the time for sleep, the hour for the tropical siesta. My five friends who have come down out of politeness to greet me have a very sleepy look. I could easily snooze for a few minutes, but where to find a little shade for my head in a country where there's not a tree, not a green bush. After some hesitation I go to ask the old chief a moment's hospitality, crawling on all fours into his lodging. The place is very warm and encumbered with stretched out bodies.

Under this turtle shell which is exactly like an overturned canoe the chief lives with his family: one wife, two sons, a daughter, a son-in-law, a grandson, plus rabbits and chickens and seven mean cats of elongated shape. They seem unusually tall on their legs. They have produced numerous kittens. They make room for me on the carpet of woven reeds. Politely people creep out noiselessly to go somewhere else to sleep, leaving me guarded by Atamou who fans me with a black feather fly chaser. And I go to sleep.

A half hour later when I came back to life, I was all alone amid a silence during which I could hear the distant roar of the surf on the coral reefs, and from time to time a short gust of the trade wind ruffling the reeds of the roof. Waking like that in the savages' dreary nest I felt a feeling of extreme homesickness. I felt far away, further away than ever and lost. And I was taken with that extreme anguish which comes with island sickness and no place in the world would have given it me so acutely as right here, the immensity of the austral seas round about me which suddenly upsets me, the violence of the feeling is almost physical.

By the hole which serves as a door, a ray of sunshine penetrates into the hut, dazzling, seen from the corner where I am stretched out. It projects the shadow of the idol that guards the entrance and the awkward shadows of two cats with unnecessarily long ears who dream sitting on their hunkers and looking out. Even this streak of light and its mournful glare seemed to have something strange about it and infinitely long ago. In this ray of sunlight in this silence this gust of tropical wind an unspeakable sadness comes to engulf my wakening; perhaps it is the sadness of the first human ages which has confusedly remained in the earth I'm stretched out on, and which again and again has warmed this hour with the same eternal sun. . . .

Understand this feeling passes fast, fleeting as a child's caprice before the full return of consciousness. Without stirring yet I'm amusing myself checking the details of the hut while the mice in spite of the two sentinel cats go quietly about their business.

The roof of reeds which shelters me is sustained by palm branches—but where did they get them since their island is without trees and has hardly any vegetation beyond reeds and grapes. In this small space, hardly a meter and a half high by four meters

77

long a thousand things are carefully suspended; little idols of black
wood which are engraved with coarse enamelling, lances with
points of sharpened obsidian, paddles carved with human figures,
feather headdresses, ornaments for the dance or for combat and
some utensils of various shapes, of use unknown to me which all
seem extremely ancient. Our ancestors of the first ages, when they
were risking the first emergence from the caves, must have built
huts like this ornamented with similar objects: one feels here a
type of humanity infinitely primitive and one might say younger
than our twenty or thirty thousand years.

But when you think of it, all this dried out wood of their war
clubs and their gods, where does it come from? And their cats,
their rabbits? I'm willing to believe the missionaries brought them.
But the mice that stroll around the houses everywhere. I don't
suppose anybody brought them. Where did they come from? The
slightest things on this isolated island bring up unanswered questions: one is amazed that there exists a flora and fauna.

As for the inhabitants of Easter Island they came from the
west from the Polynesian archipelagos; there is no doubt of that.

In the first place that is what they tell you themselves. According to the tradition of their old men they came some centuries
ago from the oceanic island situated further east, a certain island
of Rapa which really exists and still bears the same name. It was
in memory of this distant fatherland that they named their island
Rapa Nui (Great Rapa).

This origin being admitted there is still the mystery of their
voyage and their exodus. The region of the Pacific between
America and Oceania is itself larger than the Atlantic Ocean,
the widest marine solitude, the most frighteningly desert extent
of ocean there is in our world. In the center lies Easter Island,
unique tiny and negligible like a pebble in the middle of the ocean.
Furthermore the winds aren't changeable the way they are with
us. The direction is constant and always contrary for ships coming
from Polynesia with simple canoes after how many months of
beating into the wind, with what victuals, with what inexplicable
foresight how and why could those mysterious navigators suc-
ceed in reaching this grain of sand, lost in such an immensity.
Since their arrival they must have lost all means of communication
with the rest of the earth.

But it is incontestable that these people are Polynesians. Maoris. Having become a little paler than their ancestors on account of the cloudy climate, they have retained the handsome stature, the handsome countenance so characteristic, the long oval face and the great eyes a little too close together. They have conserved too a number of the customs of their brothers far away, and especially they speak their language.

It's for me one of the unexpected charms of this island that they still speak the language of the Maoris, because I have started to study the books of the missionaries, looking forward to our arrival at Tahiti, the delights of which I've dreamed since childhood. And here for the first time in my life I can try out some of those words that resound in my ears with such a novel and melodiously barbarous sound.

The great statues. Tonight I shan't forget them the way I did this morning. My siesta over and done with I asked the first person I saw who was Atamou to please take me to the sepulchers. He understood, which seemed miraculous. I said sepulchers in Tahitian marae and on Easter Island marae because these colossi of stone, the object of our journey, ornament the places where they used to bury, under piles of stones, the great chiefs killed in battle. This name of marae the natives also give to the thousand figures of fetishes and idols that fill their reed houses and which are linked in spirit with the memory of the dead.

So we set forth. Atamou and I without trailing a procession behind us, all alone to visit the nearest marae. This is my first journey on the unknown island. Following the seashore we cross a plain covered by an odd grass, sad colored and faded in appearance.

On our road we found the ruins of a small house like the one the Dane lives in. Atamou explains it was the house of the *papa farani* French father, missionary. He stopped to tell a tale, with an excess of mimicry, a story probably very moving which I didn't understand very well; from his gestures I can imagine ambushes, men hidden behind stones, gunshots and lances thrown—what did the poor priest do to them? One never knows what degree of sudden ferocity may overwhelm a savage, ordinarily gentle and coaxing, when one of these primitive passions is aroused or some obscure superstition. We must not forget that an instinct for cannibalism smoulders at the most intimate center of the Polynesian nature, so attractive and debonair; also that off there in Oceania, the Maoris in spite of their charming manners will sometimes still eat you.

His story told, Atamou, persuaded that I had understood every word, takes me by the hand and we continue our walk.

In front of us here is a mound of brown stones like the Gallic cromlechs but formed of much more enormous blocks, it dominates; on one side the sea where nothing passes; on the other the desolate plain limited in the distance by extinct craters. Atamou assures me that this is the marae and the two of us climb up on the stones.

One would say a cyclopean platform half hidden by a mass of collapsed columns, irregular and roughly carved. I'm asking for statues which I can't see anywhere. Atamou, with a curious gesture, points down at my feet. I was perched on the chin of one of them which lying on its back stared at me through the two holes that served him for eyes. I hadn't imagined it so large and formless but to tell the truth, I hadn't noticed it at all. There must have been ten of them lying on their backs half broken. Some last quake of the adjacent volcanoes without a doubt shook them down and the noise of their fall must have been terrible. Their faces were carved with an infantine lack of experience. Arms and hands are hardly indicated along the round bodies which gives them the air of pillars in a building. But you can imagine the religious terror they caused when they were all standing, straight and colossal along the shores of this ocean without ships and without limits. Atamou confirms the fact that there are others in the distant parts of the island, many others, a whole tribe downed and dead along the coral-whitened shores.

At the feet of the marae is a small circular beach surrounded by rocks. Crumbled by the sea all sorts of corals produce a sand of snowy whiteness, sowed over with delicate shells and tiny branches of a rosecolored coral.

The trade wind puffs up in gusts the way it did yesterday as the day advances. It pushes in drives in again through the solitudes of the austral sea a dense cover of clouds that makes the day darken to the point where the mountain the old cold volcanoes stand out clear against a suddenly dark sky and Atamou who sees rain coming, hurries us home.

Half way a heavy shower catches us while a furious wind flattens the grass on the plain; we stop for shelter under some rocks that form a vault. There we find ourselves in the middle of a swarm of small red moths. And the butterflies, white and yellow butterflies; who was it who brought their spawn across eight hundred leagues of ocean?

Very fast the wind carries off the swarm of clouds to continue their course over the ocean after watering the mysterious island as they pass. When we return in a hurry to the place where our frigate is anchored it is in a burst of evening sunshine.

The environs of this bay where the reed houses are grouped have at this moment an atmosphere of life and joy for all the officers have been ashore during the afternoon, each one escorted by a little troop of natives and now as the time grows near to go back aboard ship they await the arrival of the ship's dinghies, sitting on the ground amid the grownup primitive children who were their friends for the day and who are singing to give the moment a most festival air. I take my place and immediately my particular friends come running to squeeze in beside me. Petro, Houga, Marie and pretty Iouaritai. Our presence of a few hours has alas, cast a certain amount of ridicule on the masquerade that covers a people in bitter desolation. We have almost all of us exchanged, for fetishes or for arms, any kind of old clothes, in which the men with tattooed limbs have childishly decked themselves out. And most of the women have—for decency or to show off —put on miserable Mother Hubbards of discolored Indian stuffs which the priests must have, years ago, presented to their mothers which have slept long years carefully hung under the reed roofs.

They sing maoris: they all sing clapping their hands as if to mark the rhythm of a dance. The women emit notes as soft and fluted as bird songs. The men occasionally sing falsetto with trembly little voices and occasionally emit cavernous sounds like the growling of bored wild beasts. Their music is composed of short and heavily emphasized phrases, which they end by lugubrious vocalizations descending into minor key. One would say that these express the amazement of being alive, the sadness of life, and still it is joy that they sing, in the childish pleasure of seeing us, and the amusement of the little objects we have brought.

The pleasure of a day which tomorrow when we have gone will give way to monotony and silence. Prisoners in their island without trees and without water these savage singers belong to a race condemned and which, even there in Polynesia in their mother oceans, is extinguishing itself very fast. They belong to a dying segment of humanity; their singular destiny is to disappear very soon.

While they clap and amuse themselves mixed so familiarly with us other types observe us with thoughtful immobility. On the rocks that form an amphitheatre, which rises above us facing the sea appears a whole different part of the population, more fearful or more suspicious, with whom we have not been able to make friends. These are heavily tattooed men, crouching ferociously with their hands joined across their knees; and women seated in statuesque poses with whitish cloaks around their shoulders. On their hair knotted behind they wear flowered crowns of reeds. Not a movement, not a manifestation. They are content to look at us from above and from a distance. And when we move away in our ship's dinghies the setting sun already at the edge of the horizon shines on them, through tatters in the banks of clouds, with a reddish light. It shines only on their silent groups on their rock, standing out in light against the dark sky and the brown craters.

Since I'm on duty that night I run through the admiral's documents on Easter Island's history since it was discovered by "civilized" men. It was the civilized, I discovered without much surprise, who showed the most shameless savagery towards the savages.

Around 1850 a band of Peruvians thought to send out a fleet to shanghai slaves; the Maoris defended themselves as best they could, spears and stones against the muskets of the aggressors. They were defeated, it goes without saying, a great number were killed and hundreds carried off into slavery in Peru. At the end of several years the Peruvian government sent those home who were not already dead from ill treatment and homesickness. The exiles' returning home brought back smallpox and about half of the remaining population died of this new disease against which the island's sorcerors knew no remedy.

January 5

Today again we got from the commandant, one of my comrades and I, a dinghy to take us to the island in the early morning. We leave the ship at dawn. The same wind as yesterday. The trade wind straight in our faces which makes it hard to row and wets us from head to foot. Not without difficulty we reach the shore having lost our way among the coral reefs where the waves break sharper than ever. The reefs are covered with white foam which makes them hard to distinguish.

Atamou and my friends of yesterday come running to receive us and with them some savages we don't know and from them acquire a god in ironwood with a small ferocious countenance, waving black plumes on his head.

It is the first time my comrade has been able to go ashore. I take him to see the antique marae. Today we are going to try to carry off a statue. A great troop followed us this morning across the wet grass of the plain, and once arrived they start to dance like dervishes, lightfooted with their hair blowing out in the wind, naked and reddish, delicately tinted blue by their tattooing, their slender bodies moving against the brown stones and the black horizons; they dance, they dance over the enormous figures, placing their toes against the faces of the monsters, kicking them noiselessly in the nose and cheeks. I can't understand what they are singing in the constant racket of the gusts of wind and the surf.

The people of Rapa Nui, who venerate so many fetishes and little gods, seem to have no respect for the tombs. They don't remember the dead sleeping below them.

We returned to the now familiar bay where the reed huts are. There I circulate in a less formal manner than yesterday now with a small procession of my intimate friends like someone already accepted as belonging to the place.

Current opinion now admits that the Easter Island statues were not the work of the Maoris, but the work of another earlier race now unknown. This may be true of the huge statues of Rano

Raraku of which I shall speak later. But the numerous statues that used to ornament the marae along the beaches would seem to belong to the Maori race and to represent "the spirit of the sands" and "the spirit of the rocks."

A change has come over the way I am treated. Men only touch my hand and pass on. "Ia ora na taio" (good morning friend) say the chieftainess and her daughter who are working in the field digging sweet potatoes, and don't interrupt their labor.

The old chief received me in a cave near his dwelling where he spends his life crouching with his hands joined on his knees. Blue with tattooing, his body striped with dark blue, with his long hair, his long teeth and his habit of sitting still in some animal posture he would be hideous to look on if it weren't for the extreme gentleness of his eyes. He doesn't seem much interested in me any more and I cut my visit short.

Wanting to carry off one of the headdresses made of black plumes, a meter wide, which I saw on the heads of several elderly people hard to address, I open up to Houga, who is the one who understands best my hesitant phrases, and he introduces me into several houses where old men with blue faces and white teeth sit motionless as mummies. At first they don't seem to know that I'm there. One of the two is occupied. He is pulling the teeth out of a human jaw to replace the enamelled eyes of his god. There are, indeed, hanging from the ceiling large crowns of feathers but the old men demand crazy prices—my white duck trousers and my midshipman's vest with its gold trim—my new and only vest since I sold the old one yesterday. Too high, I have to give up. And Houga seeing me desolate proposes that for this evening I take a slightly old coiffure he has at his house which he'll let me have for the trousers alone. I accept this deal.

Now we must make the visit I promised yesterday to the old Danish Crusoe.

The surroundings of the little house are heartbreaking, with the semblance of a verandah there is the semblance of a little garden where grow a few meager plants from seed that must have been imported. What an exile for this man who in this almost empty countryside has not a grove of trees, not a patch of verdure to repose the eye. And in case of distress or sickness or menace of death, no way of communicating with the rest of the world.

He left at dawn to shoot rabbits, explained his morganatic spouse, inviting us with a thousand graces to come in just the same: a somewhat faded Maori of a certain age. She is naturally the grande elegante of the island. This morning she is wearing a tunic of yellow muslin with a travelling blanket of red wool thrown over her shoulders like a shawl. She offers us fresh clean water from a water jug, a rare sight because there are no springs on Rapa Nui; the natives collect water when it rains which corrupts quickly, or else fetch it from the bottoms of the craters from lakes that are often brackish. And to think that it is impossible for this man to do any better for himself, even by wishing, for there is nothing anywhere.

Hermits, now, recluses can always if fear takes hold of them go ask for help; but this one . . . my soul shivers at the mere thought of what the rainy twilight must be for him, nightfall in bad weather, winter evenings . . .

We don't want to abuse the lady's hospitality especially as it might turn out badly for one of us or even both of us so, at our rowing crew's meal time we go back aboard. There we find the preparations for carrying off the statue well under way, the admiral having decided to take the statue aboard today. Once loaded we shall leave immediately for Oceania.

By noon the expedition is ready to carry off the great idol. In the frigate's launch enormous beams have been put together in a sort of improvised chariot with a work gang of a hundred men under orders of the ship's lieutenant. But I'm on duty aboard ship and I contemplate sadly all these people leaving.

At the last moment the admiral who considers me his chief midshipman calls me to his quarter gallery. He will postpone my duty till tomorrow if I will bring him an exact sketch of the marae before its appearance is changed. It's amazing how on this whole cruise knowing how to draw has brought me permission to run on shore. I jump joyfully into the launch already full of people, where the sailors look as if they were bound for a fete.

Having loaded, the launch has trouble getting through a new passage which will bring us ashore near the marae. We reach the beach all the same but worried about the return trip. With the weight of the idol added we'll certainly have to make two trips to bring back all the sailors.

The natives are crowding in a mass on the beach and receive us with piercing cries. Since yesterday when the news got about of the plan to carry off the statue people have been arriving from all sides; people have really arrived from La Pérouse Bay on the other side of the island. Thus we see many new faces. The ship's lieutenant who commands the work gang wants the men to march towards the marae in ranks. The trumpets sound. This music they have never heard before puts the whole people into a state of indescribable joy. It becomes difficult to keep them in order, especially the sailors with all these handsome half naked women cavorting around them. Somehow having managed to finish my sketch for the admiral in the crush, I lost interest in the embarkment of the massacred statue. With my faithful Atamou, Petro, Marie and Iouaritai I return to the bay where the reed houses are to see how the repairs are going on my crown of feathers which Houga promised to complete this very evening.

I find him hard at work as I hoped, the splendid little savage. He has cut off the tail of a black rooster to replace the worn feathers. As the work advances the thing really begins to look fine. When I pass in front of his grotto the old chief calls to me by signs with an engaging confidential air. He shows me a dark powder which he has in a sheaf of dead leaves which he calls tatoo and since I seem to appreciate the industry of Rapa Nui he proposes, in exchange for my trousers, to make some slight blue designs on my legs. Another old man joins him to exchange for a box of Swedish matches a pair of earrings made from the dorsal spine of a shark. This afternoon again I'll carry off a mass of astonishing things.

Dominating this bay which has become one center of operations rises the crater of Rano Kao, the widest and possibly the most regularly shaped in the whole world. Seen from the sky it must give the effect that telescopes record on the moon. It is an immense colosseum where you could easily maneuver a great army. The last king of Rapa Nui is supposed to have climbed up there to save himself and his people at the time of the Peruvian invasion and there the great massacre took place. The footpaths are full of bones and whole skeletons still appear half lost in the grass.

At the moment of the sun's last setting I have gone back to sit on the spot where we have gotten the habit of waiting for the arrival of the dinghies. Perhaps for the last time: for I can see the launch returning on board and amid a swarm of whiteclad sailors the great brown head of the idol they are carrying off with them; the maneuver must have terminated successfully and we have a chance to leave tomorrow, too bad I'm telling myself. I'd gladly have stayed longer.

But during the evening at the moment of turning into my hammock I am called to the commandant's and I foresee something new for the following day. He announces that our departure has been postponed twenty-four hours. Tomorrow he plans to go with a group of officers to the most distant part of the island where idols far different from those we know are still standing on their own bases. The trip will be long and painful. On the map which we examined together, it amounts as a crow flies taken with a compass to six leagues, but may well amount to six or seven including detours, climbs, descents etc.; and the same to come home. He asks me if I want to come. I don't need to say that I'm dying to go but tomorrow I'm on duty, alas, we have roamed ashore all day today. I'll fix it with the admiral, says the commander. He adds laughing "One condition." "Of course yes, I'll draw statues for everybody from every side—as many as you want if you'll take me along."

January 6

Before four in the morning under a dead black night under a soupy sky we leave the frigate. Before day we reach the beach choosing a difficult and gloomy spot to land so as not to alert the natives who certainly would want to follow us. We are four from the general staff, two officers, the commander and I; the old Dane and a trusted Maori to guide us and three sailors accustomed to walking follow with their breakfast and ours hoisted on their shoulders. From the direction of the huts we can see lights shining through the grass.

We passed near the marae we devastated yesterday. Its aspect is sinister. The sky is covered with overcast except one long tear along the eastern horizon where a streak of yellow glow announces the end of night.

In single file through the wet grass we head for the interior of the island which we'll have to cross from one side to the other and after a half hour's walking the sea and the lights of the frigate disappear from our sight. We are further isolated. We are entering that central part of the island which is covered on the commandant's map by the word *Tekaonhangaroa* written in thick letters in the handwriting of the bishop of Tahiti. Tekaonhangaroa is the first name the Polynesians applied to this country. More even than Rapa Nui the word resounds with simple savagery of sound and darkness.

Even when the population was numerous the central territory seems to have been uninhabited. Something of the sort happens in the other regions peopled by Maoris who are a race of sailors and fishermen living off the sea. So in the central part of Tahiti and of Nuke in spite of admirable vegetation and forests full of flowers, have never ceased to be silent deserts. But here in Rapa Nui no forests, no trees, nothing; naked plains funereally dotted with little piles of stones. You would say an endless cemetery.

Day breaks but the sky remains sombre. A fine rain is falling and without having changed much our horizon is still closed by craters all alike with the same conical form and the same brownish coloration.

We are up to our knees in wet grass. The grass too is always the same; it covers the island to its whole extent. It's a rough kind of a plant of a grayish green, with tough branches garnished with imperceptible violet flowers. From it rise millions of those little insects we call may flies in France. As for the pyramids we ran into at every step, they are built of raw stones merely balanced one on top of the other; time has blackened them—they look as if they had been there for centuries.

All the same here is a valley where the vegetation changes a little. One imagines heath and wild sugar cane. Thin looking bushes of mimosa and also a few short trees that the officers recognize as of varieties they have seen in Oceania. There they become real trees. Did man have them brought in or have they lived here since the great mystery of the origins and then why have they stayed in this shape in this unique corner instead of developing and spreading out like the others?

At last near half-past nine, having crossed the island in its widest place we see, again deployed before us, blue reaches of the Pacific. The rain stops, the clouds tear away. The sun comes out. Really leaving Tekaonhangaroa is like awakening from a nightmare of darkness and rain.

And even in the distance near the sea we see something that looks like a European house. Our Danish Crusoe tells us it is the third habitation the old time missionaries built at a place called Vaihou. In those days there was a happy tribe living on the beach, today no one. Vaihou is a desert and the little house is a ruin. We can already see the crater of Rano Raraku at the foot of which perhaps we will find the promised statues different from all the others, stranger and still standing. At two leagues this will be the end of our journey—we will soon be there. Meanwhile we stop for breakfast in the empty house, to relieve the backs of our sailors, and then we will also have the shelter of a remnant of the roof.

A female savage very old and hideously ugly appears in the door and comes towards us with a timid smile. She's the only living thing we have seen on our path. She must have taken refuge in the ruined building. Undoubtedly she is a daughter of the vanished tribe. But how does she live? What does she eat? Roots and lichens probably and fish she catches along the shore.

After leaving Vaihou we cross a mass of footpaths worn and trodden as if a great crowd passed over it every day. This in full desert. People had told us about this and our native guide assures us that outside of this old woman there is not a human being within five leagues in any direction. . . . In this island everything is set to stir the imagination.

The place we are approaching must have been, in the night of the past, some center of adoration temple or necropolis. Now the whole region is encumbered with ruins, with terraces of cyclopean walls, the debris of fantastic constructions. And the grass, now, higher and higher, covers the traces of these mysterious times, a grass with long stiff branches like the branches of broom always the same grass of the same discolored green. . . .

We are now walking parallel to the sea along the beaches, on the cliffs there are terraces made of enormous stones. In the old days you climbed up to them by steps like those on the ancient Hindu temples. They formed the bases for heavy idols today all turned topsy turvy, their faces buried in the rubble. Spirit of the Beaches or Spirit of the Rocks, both guardians of the island against the invasion of the sea these are the actors in the ancient Polynesia the agonies which the statues illustrate.

It's here in the midst of the ruins that the missionaries discovered a number of wooden tablets engraved with hieroglyphics. The bishop of Tahiti owns some of them right now, and without doubt if someone can translate them they will give the word about the great enigma of Rapa Nui.

The gods keep multiplying as we advance towards Rano Raraku. They grow larger. We measure some ten and even eleven meters high cut from a single block. We don't only find them at the foot of the terraces, the ground is paved with them. Their formless brown masses emerge from the high grass. Their headdresses which were turbans of a sort are made of a different kind of lava of a sanguine red; they rolled in all directions when the statues fell. They look like monstrous mill wheels.

Near one tumulus a mass of jaw bones and calcined skulls seem to testify to human sacrifices over a long period. And—another mystery—paved roads like Roman roads seem to head shoreward until they are lost in the sea.

Skulls, jawbones we find everywhere. It seems impossible to scratch the ground without stirring those human remains. The country seems an immense ossuary. This comes from an epoch of which the terror is still handed down by the old people; the people of Rapa Nui knew the horror of being too numerous of starving and stifling on their island which they did not know how to leave; there followed among the tribes great waves of extermination and cannibalism. This was a period when white men didn't even suspect the existence of Oceania. During the last century, when Vancouver passed he found on the island which still had two thousand inhabitants, traces of entrenched camps on all the hills and the remains of fortifications and palisades around the craters.

So many squared stones moved, transported and erected testify to the presence here during centuries of a powerful race accustomed to the working of stone and having inexplicable methods of execution. In the origins perhaps all peoples have gone through this megalithic stage during which they controlled forces which we know nothing about.

The island seems small in proportion to this considerable zone occupied by monuments and idols. Could it have been a sacred island to which people came from afar for religious ceremonies, during the very distant epoch of Polynesian splendor, when the kings of the archipelagos had war canoes capable of affronting storms at sea and when from all parts of the great ocean they assembled in caves to take council in a secret language. . . . Or is this country a remnant of some submerged continent like Atlantis? These roads that disappear under the sea might indicate that; but the Maori legends don't mention anything of the sort and while Atlantis has formed in sinking a gigantic under sea plateau here around Easter Island is a region of unfathomable depths.

We find ourselves taken with a special fatigue and a special sort of anxiety caused by this endless walking in single file through the high grass along the narrow footpaths the savages have left in the midst of such desolation, mystery and silence. We already know these fallen statues which we meet at every step, each one exactly like the last, all of the same form, the same cast of countenance.

We ask our guide for the other statues we had come to see the different ones which are still upright.

"In just a minute," he tells us, "on the flanks of Rano Raraku is where we will find them and only there is a unique group."

The paths now turn in from the seashore towards the interior in the direction of the volcano.

About an hour and a half after our halt at Vaihou we begin to distinguish, upright on the slope, great personages that throw outlandish shadows on the mournful grass. They are planted without order. They are looking our way as if they wanted to know who was coming. Others of the long profiles with pointed noses are looking in other directions. This time it is the real thing. These are the people we are coming to visit, our patience has been rewarded. Involuntarily we lower our voices as we approach them.

It's a fact. They do not resemble the sleeping figures, lying by legions along our way. Maybe they belonged to a more distant period. They are the work of less childish artists who knew how to give them an expression. They frighten. They really don't have any bodies. They are colossal heads leaving the earth at the end of long thin necks, craning their necks as if to look into the depth of empty distances. What human race do they represent, with their pointed noses and their thin lips that show a pout of disdain or mockery. No eyes only deep cavities under the forehead and a vast and noble curve of eyebrows—and all the same, they have the look of observing and thinking. On each side of their cheeks shapes emerge that may well represent headdresses like the sphynx's headgear, or maybe it is ears spread out flat. Their width varies by five to eight meters. Some of them wear neckpieces made of incrustations of obsidian or engraved tattoo marks.

It doesn't seem likely that these are the work of Maoris. According to the tradition conserved by the old people they were earlier than the arrival of their own ancestors. The migrants from Polynesia, on landing from their canoes ten thousand years ago found the island deserted, guarded only by these monstrous visages. What race, today disappeared without leaving any other trace in human history could have lived here in ancient times and how did they become extinct?

And who will say how old these gods are? Gnawed by lichens they seem to have the patina of fifty centuries like our celtic menhirs. . . . Some have fallen and broken up, others with time and the crumbling of the mountain have been buried to the nose, seeming to sniff the earth.

The meridian sun blasts them, the tropical sun which exaggerates their harsh expression, putting more black in their sockets and the relief of their foreheads. The slope of the terrain makes their shadows long on this graveyard grass. In the sky the last tatters of cloud are melting into a violent and magnificent blue. The wind has dropped; everything has become tranquility and silence around these ancient idols; when the trade wind is quiet what would trouble the funereal tranquility of this spot lying under its uniform pall of grass because there is never anybody there and there exists on the island no beast or bird or snake, nothing but white butterflies and the muted grumbling of flies. We are half way up the mountain, here under the smiles of these great stone countenances, on the slope of the extinct crater, under our feet the deserted plain paved with statues and ruins, and for horizon the infinities of an ocean almost eternally without ships.

These dreamy groups looking so stiff in the sunlight quick, quick. I have, since I've promised, drawn them all in my album while my companions slept in the grass. And my haste, my feverish haste in noting every aspect—in spite of fatigue and the imperious drowsiness I have to fight off; my haste is to render more exact and stranger still the recollections that this fleeting vision left in my head.

Right away it is time to leave because the commandant is getting uneasy. With the sun completely unveiled in our faces we start back in single file along the narrow footpaths whose existence seems to me inexplicable, with always the same grass around us, always knee length or even up to our waists.

And in spite of the morning showers this grass is not even damp, nor the soil either. How can this country dry up so fast and get so dusty after a few hours in the midst of the immense marine deposits that surround it? Then too the persistence of the feeling of quiet on the island in the midst of the great ocean which seems only to moisten the coral beaches without ever overlapping a certain line. It would need nonetheless only the slightest change of level in the terrifying liquid masses to submerge this piece of nothing that holds its population of idols up into the sun's warmth. And fatigue helping, I feel that little by little, the soul of these ancient men of Rapa Nui penetrates my own whenever I contemplate the sovereign circle of the sea. All at once I understand, on their too isolated piece of land these great figures of the Spirit of the Sands and the Spirit of the Rocks hold at bay that terrible blue power. . . .

By dusk we are back in the inhabited region opposite our frigate's anchorage. The boatmen have been watching for our arrival through spyglasses and an embarcation leaves the ship to pick us up. I have just time to sit one last time opposite the sea in the fading light with my five savage friends and we are awaiting together the dinghy that will carry me off forever. They look quite shaken up by my departure and tell me sadly under the vault of clouds brought back by the evening wind several things I wish I could understand better. As for me, I feel a small heartbreak on saying goodbye. These are goodbyes forever. Between us eternity begins. The frigate's departure is fixed for six in the morning tomorrow; and certainly I shall never come back.

That night on board I have in my hands for the first time one of the hieroglyphic tablets of Rapa Nui which belongs to the commandant and which he has loaned me, one of those "talking sticks" as the Maoris call them. It is in the form of an elongated square with smoothed corners. Some primitive method must have been used to polish it—probably by the use of obsidian. The wood brought from I don't know where is very old and dried out. What a troubling and mysterious piece of wood. Its secrets will remain forever impenetrable. There are several ranks of characters engraved in the wood that give the impression of Egyptian work. There are men, animals, objects; you can imagine people seated or standing, fish, tortoises, lances. They eternalize that sacred language, unintelligible to other men, which the great chiefs talked when they took council in the caves. They had an esoteric meaning, they signified profound and hidden things that only the kings and the initiated priests could understand.

I am called. It is the admiral this evening and like yesterday and the day before yesterday I foresee that he is going to send me back once more to the sombre island.

In effect the admiral wants to possess an idol of stone with a special weight and physiognomy. He knows that his chief midshipman has frequented all the huts. He asks me if I can procure that for him, quickly at dawn tomorrow without delaying the departure of the frigate which is still set for six.

Of course I know an idol, his ideal idol in the old chief's very hut. I promise to bring it back to him before the anchors are hauled in exchange for an old dress great coat which he'll confide to me and, charmed to return once more to Rapa Nui, I get ready some phrases in Polynesian for one last supreme chat with my savage friends.

7 *January*

At four in the morning I'm on my way in the admiral's own whale boat. As luck would have it the weather is calm but dark and overcast. Since we arrived it's the same at the end of each

94

night—a dense overcast retards the sunrise on the island and on the sea. Now here I am once more returning to the bay I hadn't expected to see again. The nocturnal aspects of this shore are as fantastic as the morning of my first visit. Heavy darkness is piled on the old dead volcanoes while light gradually breaks along the shore. Here and there amid the rocks and the barely outlined huts there are fires in the grass and some dancing yellow flames. In front you can see the shadows of some savages roaming about keeping track of the cooking of some yams or other roots. As one approaches odors of smoke come to us, wild animal odors, tannery odors. And those naked forms in primitive attitudes in the glow of the fires reveal enough to plunge the spirit in a dream of old times. This must have been in some prehistoric dawn in the cloudy regions beginning to reveal the little activities of a human tribe during the stone age.

Women get about earlier than men. I'm first recognized by Marie and Iouaritai. They didn't think they would see us again either me or any of us. Cries of joy. They run to the old chief to tell him that I have to deal with him and that I'm in a hurry. He comes out of his hole. The deal suits him. In exchange for his idol which two of my sailors carry off making a chair with their hands I hand him the admiral's handsome frock coat and he promptly puts it on.

No time to lose. I must run down to the shore. In a few seconds my friends are out to see me one last time. Houga, waking in one leap, appears wrapped in a mantle of tapa cloth then I hear Atamou running behind me and then Petro the skinny little elf. These are really the last farewells, this time. In a few hours Easter Island will have disappeared forever from my eyes. And really a little friendship had come up among us perhaps from our deep differences as from our common childishness.

It's almost day before I embark in the whale boat with the idol. My fine friends remain among the rocks to follow me out of sight. Only the old chief who came down to the shore to say goodbye returns slowly to his hut—and seeing him so absurd in the admiral's frock coat from which protruded his long tattooed legs, I have the feeling of having failed in respect towards him, and in making this exchange to have committed the crime of *lèse-sauvagerie*.

VII

PAYMASTER THOMSON'S
ELEVEN BUSY DAYS

When the U.S.S. *Mohican* was slated to call at Easter Island in the winter of 1886 William J. Thomson, an eager young man who served as paymaster, made careful preparations to get the most out of his visit. He already was trying to learn the Polynesian language. During his ship's stopover in Tahiti he visited Bishop Jaussen and induced him to allow photographs to be taken of the rongo-rongo tablets he had in his possession. He was entrusted with letters and recommendations to a halfcaste known as Mr. Salmon who was herdsman and general foreman for the British concern which ran sheep on the island. Being fluent in the local language for many years, he was the guide and chief informant on the traditions, archaeology and folkways of the islanders to any European visitors who happened to come ashore. Furthermore he built up a good business sending Easter Island antiquities to Tahiti for sale.

Under his guidance Paymaster Thomson tirelessly ran over the island from one end to the other. Mr. Salmon acted as his interpreter. He visited every monument of importance, talked as much as possible with the natives and listed the plants and the fishes which he considered the islanders' chief source of food.

His report was published by the American Museum in Washington in 1889.

EXPLORATION OF THE ISLAND

The *Mohican* came to anchor in the roadstead of Hangaroa on the morning of Saturday, December 18, 1886. The individuals most interested in the exploration of the island went on shore without delay, and the work was pushed forward as rigorously as possible until the hour appointed for the sailing of the ship for Valparaiso on the evening of the last day of the year.

Messrs. Salmon and Brander boarded the ship upon her arrival and extended the hospitalities of Easter Island, placing their limited resources entirely at our command with a heartiness that won our immediate esteem, and which ripened into sincere friendship before our departure. These gentlemen are closely connected with the royal family of Tahiti, and we had been intrusted with letters and various articles from relatives and friends who desired to embrace the opportunity for communication offered by the *Mohican.*

Upon landing at Hangaroa we found nearly all of the natives on the island congregated to receive their unknown visitors. The men inspected us closely and were profuse in friendly demonstrations, while their wives and daughters gazed curiously from a little distance, and the children's manner plainly showed the enjoyment of an occasion of infrequent occurrence in their quiet lives. Surrounded by this crowd we walked about a mile to the house of Mr. Brander, where the baggage, tools, and impedimenta in general were deposited. During the afternoon a reconnaissance was made to the crater of Rano Kao and the ancient stone houses in the vicinity, and in the evening we crossed the island in a light wagon with Mr. Salmon to his residence at Vaihu. That gentleman has, during his long residence on the island, accumulated a valuable collection of curios and relics of the former inhabitants.

RECONNAISSANCE TO RANO KAO

Sunday, December 19.—Made an early start from Vaihu and rode to the central elevations called Mount Teraai, Mount Punapau, and Mount Tuatapu and inspected the quarries from whence

the red tufa was obtained which formed the crowns or headdresses that ornamented all the huge images. Following the road
to the southwest we made the ascent of Rano Kao. The crater
is nearly circular and about a mile in diameter with steep jagged
sides, or walls, except on the south, where the lava flow escaped
to the sea. A lake fills the bottom of what was once the volcanic
caldron; the water is of great depth and the surface covered with
a coat of peat, so dense and strong that cattle range over it,
finding food at irregular intervals. The surface of the lake is about
700 feet from the top, but the cattle have made a path by which
the descent can be made with safety.

Skirting the edge of the crater to the southward the ridge
becomes narrower, falling precipitously a thousand feet to the
sea on one side, and descending abruptly into the crater on the
other until it terminates in an elongated wall of rock rising to a
sharp, jagged edge impassable to either man or beast. Just where
this elevated edge contracts rapidly towards the south are located
the ancient stone houses of Orongo. These burrow-like dwellings
were built with little regard to streets, avenues, etc., but were
regulated by the contour of the land. Piles of debris in one or two
spots marked the destroying hand of former investigators, but the
large majority of the houses were intact, and in some instances
the openings had been sealed up with stone, making it difficult
to outline the original entrances. These dwellings were constructed
without windows or other openings except a door-way so low and
narrow that an entrance could only be effected by crawling upon
the hands and knees, while in many cases it was necessary to creep
serpent-like through the contracted confines. Many interiors
were inspected by the light of candles provided for the purpose
and houses marked for thorough investigation on the morrow.

While tracing and sketching the sculptured rocks in the vicinity
of Orongo, the declining sun hastened the departure for Vaihu,
where the hours after our evening meal were devoted to making
notes of the native traditions as translated by Mr. Salmon, until
that good-natured gentleman could be kept awake no longer.
It had been proposed that we should occupy one of the ancient
stone houses for the night, in order to be near the scene of operations planned for the next day, but they were damp and ill-

smelling and the work accomplished on the traditions more than repaid the time lost in recrossing the island.

THE ANCIENT STONE HOUSES AT ORONGO

December 20.—Leaving Vaihu at early daylight we arrived at Hangaroa in time to meet the detachment of eight selected men sent on shore from the ship with proper tools and implements for making a thorough exploration of Orongo and vicinity. The blue-jackets scampered up the slope of Rano Kao with the buoyant spirits of schoolboys out for a holiday, and arriving at the spot were anxious to lend the assistance of willing hands and plenty of brawn to the prosecution of the work.

Every house was entered and inspected, though occasionally a miscalculation was made in the dimensions of a narrow passage-way and it became necessary to rescue a prisoner by dragging him back by the heels. Once inside the building, the interior could be easily inspected and sketches made of frescoes and sculptured figures.

These remarkable habitations were built against a terrace of earth or rock, which in some cases formed the back wall of the dwelling. From this starting point a wall was constructed of small slabs of stratified basaltic rock, piled together without cement and of a thickness varying from about 3 feet to a massive rampart of 7 feet in width.

The outer entrance is formed by short stone posts planted in the ground and crossed by a basaltic slab. The passage-way was in all cases unpaved and usually lined on the top and both sides with flat stones. This important feature added materially to our comfort while forcing an entrance through some of the narrow openings, and saved the necessity for adding to our already boun-tiful supply of bruises and abrasions. No regularity of plan is shown in the construction of the majority of the houses; some are parallelogram in shape, others elliptical, and many are immethodi-cal, showing a total absence of design, the builder being guided by the conformation of the ground, the amount of material available, and other chance circumstances. These houses are roofed with slabs of rock of sufficient length to span the side walls, showing that no particular care had been exercised to form close joints. Over this stone ceiling the earth was piled in mound shape, reaching a depth in the center of from 4 to 6 feet, and covered by a sod that afforded ample protection from rain. The floors were the bare earth, and the interiors were damp and moldy from insufficient ventilation afforded by the single contracted opening.

The largest house contained a single chamber nearly 40 feet long; three were over 30 feet, and eight measured over 20 feet in length, with other dimensions approximately the same as the general average. These rude dwellings were not in all cases confined to a single apartment; some have one and a few have two or three recess chambers opening out of the main room; but they were dark little dens, having no separate light or ventilation.

Near the center of this assemblage of houses there is a sort of square court with eight door-ways opening upon it. These might be considered separate and distinct dwellings, though the apartments are connected by interior passage-ways, making it possible to pass from one to the other. At the extreme end of the point a similar collection of houses opens upon a circular court, and the interiors are also connected.

The majority of the houses at Orongo are in a fair state of preservation and bear evidence of having been occupied at no very remote period. The result of the investigation here showed very little of carving on stone, but the smooth slabs lining the walls and ceilings were ornamented with mythological figures and rude designs painted in white, red, and black pigments. Houses marked 1, 5, and 6 on Lieutenant Symond's chart were demolished at the expense of great labor and the frescoed slabs obtained. Digging beneath the door-posts and under the floors produced nothing beyond a few stone implements.

The houses in this vicinity occupy such a prominent position that they were naturally robbed of everything in the way of relics by the natives, who were beginning to appreciate the value of such things through the importance placed upon them by the foreign vessels that have called at the island. A niche in the wall of each of these dwellings was evidently designed to receive the household god and the various valuables which were possessed by the inhabitants. Whatever treasures they may have held in former years, we found them empty, and our search revealed nothing of importance.

Attention was directed to one of the buildings in this assemblage that apparently had no entrance way. One wall was demolished, disclosing a rude coffin containing the remains of a native recently deceased. The unoccupied house had been utilized as a tomb, and sealed up with the material of which the walls were built.

SCULPTURED ROCKS

The most important sculptured rocks on this island are in the immediate vicinity of the stone houses at Orongo. As much time as possible was devoted to examining and sketching these curious relics. The hard volcanic rock is covered by carvings intended to represent human faces, birds, fishes, and mythical animals, all very much defaced by the ravages of time and the elements. The apparent age of some of the rock carvings antedates the neighboring stone houses, the images, and other relics of the island except the ruined village on the bluff west of Kotatake Mountain. Fishes and turtles appear frequently among these sculptures, but the most common figure is a mythical animal, half human in form, with bowed back and long claw-like legs and arms. According to the natives, this symbol was intended to represent the god "Meke-Meke," the great spirit of the sea. The general outline of this figure rudely carved upon the rocks, bore a striking resemblance to the decoration on a piece of pottery which I once dug up in Peru, while making excavations among the graves of the Incas. The form is nearly identical, but, except in this instance, no similarity was discovered between the relics of Easter Island and the coast of South America.

Ancient Customs in Relation to Gathering the Sea Birds Eggs

From the most reliable information that could be obtained, the stone houses at Orongo were built for the accommodation of the natives while celebrating the festival of the "sea birds eggs," from a remote period until the advent of the most important ceremonies.

During the winter months, sea birds in great numbers visit the island to lay their eggs and to bring forth their young. The nests are made among the ledges and cliffs of the inaccessible rocks, but a favorite spot for these birds has always been the tiny islands Mutu RauKau and Mutu Nui, lying a few hundred yards from the southwest point of the island. Here the first eggs of the season are laid, and therefore Orongo was selected as a convenient point to watch for the coming of the birds. According to the ancient custom, the fortunate individual who obtained possession of the first egg and returned with it unbroken to the expectant crowd, became entitled to certain privileges and rights during the following year. No especial authority was vested in him, but it was supposed that he had won the approval of the great spirit "Meke-Meke" and was entitled to receive contributions of food and other considerations from his fellows. The race for the distinguished honor of bearing off the first egg was an occasion of intense excitement. The contestants were held in check at Orongo until the auspicious moment arrived, and the scramble commenced at the word "go," pronounced by the king, who was about the only able-bodied man on the island who did not participate. It was decidedly a go as you please race, every man selecting his route to the sea by the circuitous paths or directly over the face of the cliff, and many fatal falls are recorded as the result.

The swim to Mutu RauKau was a trifling matter, the chief difficulty being to return with an egg unbroken through the general scramble.

The houses at Orongo were probably unoccupied except for a short period in July of each year while awaiting the coming of the sea birds. The peculiarity of their construction might be accounted for by the fact that the thatched hut, common to the plains, could not be used to advantage on this exposed bluff. The low, contracted entrances, were used here as well as elsewhere for defense. Factional fights were common, and it was necessary that every house should be guarded against surprise and easily defended. Another reason might be found for making the openings as small as possible, in the absence of doors to shut out the storms. The sculptured rocks in the vicinity of Orongo bear record to the grateful contestants in the egg-races to the great spirit "Meke-Meke" for his benign influence and protection, much after the manner in which boats, pictures, and other objects are dedicated to certain patron saints in more civilized portions of the earth.

EMPLOYMENT OF NATIVES

The investigations in the vicinity of Orongo having been finished, a contract was made with Mr. Brander for removing from the excavations and transporting to the landing place the frescoed slabs, inscribed door-posts, and objects collected, and the evening was devoted to the native traditions until exhausted nature demanded a few hours rest. With a view of propitiating the natives and securing their good will and cooperation in prosecuting the work with the utmost dispatch, a number of men were employed to assist in the excavations made at Orongo, but the experiment proved a failure. They constituted themselves an appreciative audience, and could not be induced to work. They evinced a lively interest in all that was going on, and performed astounding gastronomic feats at meal time. We concluded to dispense with their services after a demonstration of their dexterity in causing the disappearance of every small object that remained unprotected for a moment. Several of the head-men, afterwards employed as guides to accompany the expedition around the island, and stimulated with the hope of bountiful rewards, performed valuable service in the way of locating water-holes, identifying localities, naming objects of interest, etc.

December 21.—Preparations were made for an early start on the expedition already planned. The native contingent was dispatched about daylight with camp equipage and instructions to form Camp Mohican at a spot where it was reported good water could be found in abundance. We were somewhat handicapped for the march by the fatigue of the last few days, added to the want of rest. The hospitality of the Brander establishment had been cordially extended, but such a large and varied assortment of insects and noxious animals had possession of the premises, that we preferred the open air, though there were several passing showers during the night. A working party from the ship, consisting of nine men, including a boatswain's mate and quartermaster, landed at an early hour, each man equipped with knapsack, canteen, shovel and pick. The expedition took the road passing through the villages of Mataveri and Hangaroa to the coast, followed by almost every man, woman, and child on the island. The interest displayed by the natives in our movements gradually died out after a few hours of hard walking, and towards noon the last party returned to their homes, leaving us a clear field.

Following the coastline to the northwest, every part of the ground was carefully examined, platforms measured and plotted, excavations made, and objects of interest collected and catalogued.

Near Anahoirangaroa Point, on some ledges of hard volcanic rock we found numerous depressions that evidently were made at the cost of great labor. Some are elliptical in shape, others perfectly circular, averaging about 3 feet in diameter and 2 feet deep. The majority are above high water line and others just awash when the tide is full. No explanation could be obtained in regard to these holes, and it was concluded that they were originally intended as live boxes for the preservation of fish.

The natives have a superstition to the effect that any one who walks over these rocks will be afflicted with sore feet, and we received many solemn warnings in regard to it. If there is any foundation for it at all, it is probably due to a succulent vine that grows here, coming in contact with the wounds caused by the sharp rocks. A short distance farther on stands a round tower 12 feet in diameter and 20 feet high, said to have been erected as a lookout station from whence the movements of turtles could be watched. We found here, as well as under every other pile of stones of any description on the island, tombs and receptacles for the dead, all filled with human remains in various stages of decay, from freshly interred bodies to the bones that crumbled into dust upon exposure to the air. The entire island seems to be one vast necropolis, and the platforms along the sea coast appear to have been the favorite burial places in all ages. Natural caves were utilized as places of deposit for the dead.

Considerable time was devoted to the examination of the platforms, and in numerous instances interesting catacombs and tombs were discovered, containing remains of great antiquity. In this connection a peculiar trait in the native character was developed. Towards evening one of the native guides returned to pilot the working party to the place selected for the camp, just at the time a particularly old tomb had been uncovered and the crania were being removed from their former resting place. This the unsophisticated native took in at a glance, and with the announcement that we were desecrating the burial place of his forefathers, he set up a howl of despair, and became prostrated with grief at the sight of a skull which he claimed to recognize as that of his great-grandfather. Notwithstanding the absurdity of the statement, the anguish displayed induced us to return the bones to their ancient resting place. The afflicted youth quickly dried his eyes, and intimated that for a suitable reward he would be willing to dispose of the remains of his ancestors, and he thought that a consideration of about $2 would assuage his grief. That settled it. The skulls were gathered into the collection, and the sorrowing native left to mourn the loss both of the money and of the bones of his forefathers.

Many of the stone bases upon which the images stood still remain in their original positions upon the platforms. Generally they are regular in shape, a few have been squared. We found one of octagon shape that stood the test of measurement very well. Between platforms that we numbered 4 and 5 the land falls away gently to the sea, and this slope is paved regularly with small round bowlders, having every appearance of having been constructed as a way for hauling out boats. The coast in this vicinity is perfectly rock bound, but a narrow channel extends from the paved way out to sea. Boats might land here at any time. With the wind southwest, or in any direction except west, the landing would be perfectly smooth. The place is admirably adapted to the landing of heavy weights, but, as far as known, the images were never transported by sea, nor did the islanders possess boats sufficiently large to float them, or material from which they could be constructed.

CAVE AND TOMB NEAR AHUAKAPU POINT

On the face of the cliff near the point, Ahuakapu, a large and interesting cave, was visited. Many of the recesses and angles had been walled up and contained human remains. Fossiliferous specimens of marine animals were obtained by digging up the floor of the cave. The igneous rocks in the vicinity show evidences of rude sculptures, among which could be traced canoes, fishes, and men in various attitudes. Upon the extreme point we found another one of those round towers, built for the purpose of observing the movements of turtles on the beach.

RUINS OF THE OLDEST HABITATION ON THE ISLAND

On the high bluff west of Kotatake Mountain we discovered the ruins of a settlement extending more than a mile along the coastline and inland to the base of the hill. These remains bear unmistakable evidences of being the oldest habitations on the island. The houses are elliptical in shape, with doorways facing the sea, and were built of uncut stone. Some of the walls are standing, but the majority are scattered about in the utmost confusion. An extremely interesting feature of these ancient ruins is the fact that each dwelling was provided with a small cave or niche at the rear end, built of loose lava stones, which was in a number of instances covered by an arch supported by a fairly shaped keystone. The recesses were undoubtedly designed to contain the household gods, and the keystone, although extremely rough in construction, is unmistakable in its application. Our guides had no knowledge of this locality and knew no distinctive name for it.

Messrs. Salmon and Brander had not visited the spot, because the location is bleak and desolate and, as far as they had heard, was a trackless waste, devoid of all interest.

Camp Mohican was formed a few hundred yards in the rear of one of the great platforms. We reached the spot just as the shades of night were closing in, footsore and weary from the hard day's march. The camp was not more than 5 miles in a direct line from our starting point in the morning, but we had traveled many times the distance in making a thorough inspection of the ground. A narrow pathway follows the coastline for a part of the distance, which affords safe footing for the natives; everywhere else the ground is covered with volcanic rocks of every conceivable size and shape, making the walking both difficult and dangerous. The site for the camp was selected because of the proximity of a water-hole, the only one to be found in this

29. They lie in a row just as they were pulled down in the stormy years after 1680

30. The seven monoliths of Akivi set back on their bases by Dr. William Mulloy in 1960

31. The crouched basalt figure against the lava wall of Rano Raraku

32. Confabulation of great heads:
Rano Raraku

33. *Moai* engraved on chest with a ship which might be built of totora reed

34. Head of statue, Rano Raraku

35. The basalt figure again

37. Apologies to Charles de Gaulle

36. (LEFT) Crouched basalt figure: one of the most powerful of ancient sculptures

38.
There is an eerie feeling of life about them.
In some lights they seem to be talking
among themselves

39. Thoughtful poses

GEORGE HOLTON, PHOTO RESEARCHERS, INC.

40. What happened to the sculptors
who dropped their basalt picks
and never came back?

41. House foundation at Anakena

42. (RIGHT) Burial place under a fallen statue

43. After a century of effort the
talking wood is still undeciphered

44. Outdoor school: now the Pascuenses have a handsome new school-
house

45. Hangaroa house

46. Inaugurating the new school

47. Woodcarver at work

48. The arrival of Father Sebastian's body

49. The burial services for Father Sebastian

neighborhood. It proved to be a shallow cave where the rain-water collected from the drainage of the surrounding hills; the fluid was full of both animal and vegetable matter and decidedly unpleasant to taste and smell. A shelter-tent was improvised by suspending a blanket at the ends from boarding pikes planted in the ground, and after a hasty meal all hands sought the much needed rest. About midnight omnious looking clouds rolled up from the southeast, and it rained in heavy squalls until morning. Wet and unrefreshed, we turned out at daylight to resume the march with everything completely saturated from underclothing to note-books, but with undaunted resolution to continue the work in spite of the elements.

NATURAL CAVES

Among some outcropping rocks near by, a cave was accidentally discovered, with a mouth so small that an entrance was effected with difficulty. Once inside, however, it branched out into spacious chambers that could shelter thousands of people with comfort. It bore evidences of having been used in former years as a dwelling-place, and probably had other entrances and extensions which we failed to penetrate for the want of time. Human remains were found in this cave, but all very old.

The caves of Easter Island are numerous and extremely interesting in character. They may be divided into two classes: those worn by the action of the waves, and those due to the expansion of gases in the molten lava and other volcanic action. The process of attrition is in constant progress around the entire coastline, and the weaker portions of the rock are being undermined by the incessant beating of the ocean. Some of these sea-worn caves are of considerable extent, but generally difficult of access and affording little of interest except to the geologist. The caverns produced by volcanic agencies are found throughout this island, and some were traced through subterranean windings to an outlet on the bluffs overlooking the sea. They are generally quite dry; the rain water falling upon the surface occasionally finds its way between the cracks or joints in the solid rock, but these gloomy passages and chambers lack grandeur from the entire absence of stalactites and deposits of carbonate of lime. No glistening and fantastical forms of stalagmitic decorations exist here to excite the fancy and create in the imagination scenes of fairy-like splendor. The feeble rays of our candles were quickly absorbed by the somber surroundings, heightening the apparent extent and gloom of the recesses. Careful investigation proved that all of the caves visited had been used as dwelling-places by the early inhabitants.

The day's march had been exceedingly fatiguing on account of the rugged nature of the ground and the absence of water, but the last mile or so was accomplished at a swinging pace in view of the fact that the camp could not be reached after darkness had closed in. Our course had been around Cape North, and covering the territory between the coast and the base of Rana Hana Kana. Loose bowlders of every imaginable shape and size cover the ground, threatening sprained limbs and broken bones at every incautious step, as though the expiring energy of the volcanoes had been expended in creating this natural barrier.

Camp Day, named in honor of our commanding officer, was located in a district known as Vai-mait-tai (good water), but it was decidedly a misnomer, the supply being ample, but brackish and ill-smelling. After a hearty meal of mutton, prepared by our guides in true island style, we sought shelter under the lee of an outcropping rock, fatigued enough to sleep through the attacks of myriads of noxious insects and regardless of the passing showers of rain.

ANAKENA BAY

December 23.—A dip in the sea at daylight, and a breakfast of mutton which had been slowly roasting all night on hot stones placed in the ground and covered with earth to prevent the escape of heat, put us in prime condition for the work in hand. Our route lay along the north coast of the island and around Anakena Bay, the place where Hotu-Matua and his followers landed when they arrived from the unknown and much-disputed locality from which they migrated. On the sand beach of this bay we found the small univalve, the remains of which were noticed in all the caves and ruins on the island and which are still highly esteemed by the natives as an article of food. Jelly-fish, such as are known to the sailors as "Portuguese men-of-war," also abound, and are esteemed a delicacy by the natives. The entire plain back of Anakena (La Pérouse) Bay is covered with small platforms, cairns, tombs, and the ruins of dwellings of various sorts. Houses built of loose stones, nearly circular in shape, are plentiful; but they belong to a comparatively recent date, as is indicated by the fact that the stones, of which they are constructed, have been taken from the platforms and from the foundations of the thatched tents. Any sort of material that came handy appears to have been freely used by the builders of these houses. In several we found well-cut heads that had formerly ornamented image platforms, built in the walls, some facing inside and others in the opposite direction. The ruins in the vicinity show that this had been the site of a large settlement, and that it continued to be a place of importance through many generations; but the greatest mystery is how such a number of people obtained a sufficient supply of fresh water.

Near Anakena is a large image in the best state of preservation of any found about the platforms of the island. The traditions assert that this was intended to represent a female, and that it was the last image completed and set up in place. Our guides informed us that it was only thrown down about twenty-four years ago, and previous to that time it had remained for many years the only statue standing upon a platform on the island. Camp Whitney was located at Hangaone Bay, where we found shelter in a bug-infested cave. The water supply was obtained from an ancient tomb nearby, and was both scant in quantity and nasty in quality. We were, however, in such an indifferent state of mind that anything wet was acceptable.

December 24.—With the knowledge that we had a particularly hard march before us, we struck camp early and got under way before it was fairly light in the morning. Around Cape Pokokoria the rugged nature of the ground passed over was extremely exhausting. The slopes of Mount Puakalika are in places covered with coarse hummock-grass and flowering vines, which look green and attractive during the rainy season of the year, but which were at this time almost as dry and parched as though scorched by fire. The toilsome march of this day was heightened by the absence of water, and all suffered severely from thirst. Starting out in the morning with empty canteens, our throats soon became dry and painful. A small quantity of water was found in the after-noon in Mount Puakalika crater, thick and unpleasant to look upon, but affording valuable relief to our sufferings.

THE POIKE PLAINS

The Poike Plains are extensive tracts of fine red volcanic sand and dust with occasional patches of hummock-grass struggling for existence in this barren waste. Manga Tea-tea (White Mountains), so called from the grayish appearance of the rocks, furnished the stone implements of the natives. The material was chipped as nearly as possible into the desired shape and then ground down to a point or edge by friction upon a hard surface with sand and water. At Anakena and other points convenient to the sand beach we found grinding stones, together with unfinished and broken implements.

The traditions assert that the island was in former ages densely populated, and the legends are supported by the gigantic works of the image and platform builders and the ruins of various sorts scattered about. While the accounts are probably greatly exaggerated in regard to the number of inhabitants at one time, there is every reason to believe that the people were numerous enough to severely tax for their support the limited area of ground available for cultivation. The Incas of Peru usually selected for burial-places the rocky and steep slopes of the hills or the low sandy plains, where cultivation was impossible, and presuming that a similar economy might have been practiced here, much time was devoted to a thorough examination of the sand-wastes at the eastern extremity of the island. Excavations were made at the expense of great labor in several places where the indications were most promising, but with barren results. Digging to a depth of 9 feet in a depression near Cape Anataavanui we found several flat stones of large size, such as were used for facing the platforms, but the loose, shifting nature of the sand made it impossible for our small force to thoroughly investigate them. The trade winds freely sweep these elevated plains, blowing the sand about, and creating ridges that may be leveled again by stronger currents at some other season. Hills and depressions simply represent the force and direction of the wind at the time.

TONGARIKI

Camp Baird was delightfully located in a commodious cave called Ana Havea, on the bay of Hanga Nui, near Point Onetea, and convenient from its proximity to Rano Raraku where all the monoliths on the island had been quarried. Tongariki with its rich remains of platforms, images, cairns, and tombs, and Vaihu and other points not yet explored, were sufficient to induce a permanent establishment during the remainder of our stay at Easter Island. The cave was dry, with spacious entrance exposed to the full force of the trade winds, and we were comfortable to a degree, after dried grass and bulrushes had been collected to sleep upon. Successive generations of natives probably occupied this ancient cavern; an extensive corral has been built near by, and Messrs. Salmon and Brander sleep here while rounding up their cattle. Drinking water, the great desideratum on the island, obtained from sources that form the crater of Rano Raraku, was, owing to its animal and vegetable impurities, unpalatable, while the supply from the springs was more so, but afforded a pleasing variety, which enabled us to exercise a preference for some other, whenever either kind was used. The so-called springs are holes into which the sea-water percolates, and are as salt as the ocean, at high tide, and decidely brackish at all other stages.

December 25.—The forenoon was devoted to the exploration of the face of the bluff to the eastward of Tama Point. Many caves were reached after difficult and dangerous climbing, and were found to contain nothing of interest, while others of traditional importance were inaccessible from below, and we were not provided with ropes and the necessary appliances for reaching them from above. No doubt there are caves in this vicinity with contracted entrances that have been covered by loose rocks and intentionally concealed. One such cavern was found by accident. It contained a small image about 3 feet high, carved out of hard gray rock. It was a splendid specimen of the work and could be easily removed to the boat-landing at Tongariki. Retracing our steps toward the camp, the ground between Puakalika elevation and Rano Raraku was thoroughly examined during the afternoon. The plain is completely covered with cairns, tombs, and platforms.

Many of the most promising were completely demolished and the foundations dug up to a depth of six feet. All contained human remains in various stages of decay, and the earth upon which they were built proved to be a rich loam filled with sea shells of minute size, free of stones, while outside of the foundation walls the composition was composed of bowlders of all sizes with very little earth. Among the vast ruins are many fragments of images and crowns scattered about, and it is evident that platforms were erected and destroyed by succeeding generations. The traditions assert, and appearances indicate, that this plain had from the earliest times been one of the most densely populated districts on the island. Only the remains of walls and cisterns were found here. They were generally small, the largest being 9 feet in diameter, 14 feet deep, and surrounded by a sloping bank paved with small stones to facilitate the collection of rain water.

In honor of the day, work was suspended earlier than usual, and we returned to camp a couple of hours before sundown, but we found that our Christmas cheer had been reduced to "hard-tack" and island mutton by the *léger-de-main* of our native assistants, though ample stores had been provided for the entire expedition. With no indulgence in indigestible Christmas luxuries, we were enabled to retire to an undisturbed rest at an earlier hour than would have been probable in a more civilized land and with different surroundings.

December 26.—Our native contingent deserted in a body at daylight on the plea that their religious convictions would not permit them to work on Sunday. Remonstrances and arguments were in vain, and we had to permit them to depart after exacting a promise that they would return early the next morning. Luka, the chief guide, lingered a while to state that his family burial place was beneath the great platform of Tongariki, and that he had a decided aversion to having the skulls of his ancestors added to our collection.

Sunday inspection and its attendant functions has through long custom become second nature with the men who have been long in the service, and through the desire to thus mark the day, the most valuable of our geological specimens were lost. The boat-swain's mate took advantage of our temporary absence to clean up the cave and make it more presentable, and, in doing so, threw all the stones and "trash" into the sea. Nothing could be said, in view of the fact that it was done with the best possible intentions, but he was greatly chagrined to find that those same stones had been carried over many a weary mile to be lost now, when it was impossible to obtain duplicates or other specimens of some of the peculiar formations met with on the first days of the trip.

RANO RARAKU

The day was devoted to the examination of the inside of the crater of Rano Raraku. The walls of the crater are very abrupt except on the west side, where the lava-flow escaped to the sea, and here the cattle and horses find easy access to the pool of water that has collected in the bottom. High up on the southern side are the workshops of the image-builders, extending in irregular terraces quite to the top. Here we found images in all stages of incompletion, from the rude outline drawing to the finished statue ready to be cut loose from its original rock and launched down the steep incline. The *modus operandi* appears to have been to select a suitable rock upon which the image was sketched in a reclining position. The upper surface having been carved into shape and entirely finished, the last work was to cut the back loose from the rock. This necessitated the exercise of great care to prevent the breaking off of exposed portions, and was accomplished by building piles of stones to sustain the weight while it was being undermined.

Ninety-three statues in all were counted inside the crater, and of these forty are standing up, completed and ready to be transported to the platforms for which they were intended. They stand well down towards the bottom of the slope, and are more or less buried in the earth by the washings from above.

The work of lowering the huge images from the upper terraces to the bottom of the crater and thence over the wall and down into the plain below, was of great magnitude, and we are lost in wonder that so much could be accomplished by rude savages ignorant of everything in the way of mechanical appliances. The average weight of these statues would be something between 10 and 12 tons, but some are very large and would weigh over 40 tons. It is possible that a slide was made, upon which the images were launched to the level ground below; a number of broken and damaged figures lie in a position to suggest that idea, but from the bottom of the crater they were transported up and over the wall and thence over hill and dale to various points all over the island. Excavations were made at different points inside the crater, but nothing was found of interest beyond a few broken stone implements that had no doubt been used by the image-builders.

December 27.—We made an early start and visited the image-builders' workshops on the west side of Rano Raraku, which are much more extensive than those on the inside of the crater. These workshops commence well up on the side of the mountain and extend quite to the summit by irregular terraces. In places these terraces extend one above another with unfinished images upon each, and the configuration of the land is such as to preclude all idea of launching the statues by means of a slide. We were unable to arrive at any satisfactory conclusion as to how the immense statues on the upper tier of works could be moved to the plain below, passing over the underlying cavities where similar works had been quarried. We know the natives had ropes made of hemp, two kinds of which are indigenous to the island, but it is difficult to conjecture how these heavy weights were handled without mechanical appliances. One hundred and fifty-five images were counted upon this slope in various stages, including those standing at the base of the mountain finished and complete, ready for removal to the platforms. Many of the images in the workshops are of huge proportions, but the largest one on the island lies on one of the central terraces in an unfinished condition and measures 70 feet in length, 14 1/2 feet across the body; the head being 28 1/2 feet long. Some of the standing statues are in as perfect condition as the day they were finished.

One is noticeable from the fact that the head is slightly turned to one side and is known as the "wry-neck," but whether it is the result of accident or design could not be determined.

Another excellent specimen of these remarkable figures stands near the last mentioned and shows tool-marks around the neck as though an effort had been made to cut the head off. The natives call this "hiara" and have a tradition to the effect that it belonged to a powerful clan who were finally defeated in war, and that their enemies had made an attempt to destroy the statue by cutting off the head. The story may be based only upon the mutilation, but the chances are that it is founded upon fact.

Nothing of importance was found by digging about the images or in the workshops except broken stone implements which had been used by the builders. In one of the quarries we found the only trace of sculptured figures in the vicinity.

These emblems were carved upon a smooth rock over a half-finished image.

December 28.—Shortly after daylight the entire force started making excavations under the foundations of the image-builders' houses, the ruins of which extend towards Rano Raraku from Tongariki Bay, on regular terraces. These peculiar ruins are to be found here in great numbers both inside and outside of the crater, but do not differ from those already described. A custom obtained among the islanders, similar to that practiced by the tribes of Alaska and other Indians of America, of burying something of interest or value beneath the door posts of their dwellings. Usually it was a smooth beach pebble which was supposed to have some fetish qualities to bring good luck or ward off evil influences.

One of the largest of these ruins has an extensively paved terrace in front. At a depth of about three feet below the surface of the central door-way, we found a rough angular flinty stone with a rudely carved face upon it. A prominent ruin of the same description inside of the crater, and another near the workshop on the outside, yielded a hard stone upon which marks had been carved very similar to those on the rocks at Orongo.

SKULLS SHOWING PECULIAR MARKS

One of our guides produced from a hiding place three ancient skulls, described elsewhere, upon the top of which these same mystical figures had been cut. They were not shown until a reward had been promised, and the guide claimed to have obtained them in their present condition from the King's platform.

On the outside of the crater of Rano Raraku, near the top and looking towards the southwest, we found a workshop containing fifteen small images. These had been overlooked in our former trips to this place.

Scattered over the plains extending towards Vaihu are a large number of images, all lying face downward. The indications are that they were being removed to their respective platforms when the work was suddenly arrested. These heavy weights were evidently moved by main strength, but why they were dragged over the ground face downward instead of upon their backs, thus protecting their features, is a mystery yet unsolved. One statue in a group of three is that of a female; the face and breast is covered with lichen, which at a short distance gives it the appearance of being whitewashed.

December 29.—We continued the work of exploration of Vaihu around the southwest points of the island. Excavations were made wherever the indications were good, but the results did not differ from those already described. Mount Orito was visited, from whence the obsidian was obtained for spear-heads, and also the quarries that produce the red pigment from which the natives make a red paint by rubbing it down with the juice of the sugarcane. The remainder of the stay on Easter Island was devoted to the collection of traditions, translations of tablets, and similar matters of interest.

Language

The principal feature of interest, connected with Easter Island, is the written language by which the ancient traditions and legends were perpetuated. The existence of the incised tablets was not known until the missionaries settled upon the island. Numerous specimens were found in the possession of the natives, but no especial attention appears to have been directed towards them. Several persons, belonging to vessels that were wrecked at Easter Island, report having seen these tablets, but they were so highly prized by the natives, that they could not be induced to part with them. The three hundred islanders who emigrated to Tahiti had in their possession a number of these tablets; they created some attention on account of the remarkable skill with which the figures were executed, but they were highly prized by the owners and no effort was made to secure them because their real value was not discovered. The Chilean corvette *O'Higgins* visited

Easter Island in January, 1870, and Captain Gana secured three tablets, two of which are on deposit in the nation museum at Santiago de Chile and the third was sent to France, but does not appear to have reached its destination. Paper impressions and casts were taken from the Chilean tablets for the various museums of Europe. Those sent to the English Ethnological Society created some interest after a time, but others sent to Berlin were regarded as stamps for marking native cloth (Mittheilungen, July, 1871). Seven of these tablets are now in the possession of Tepano Jaussen, bishop of Axieri, all in an excellent state of preservation.

While the *Mohican* was at Tahiti, the bishop kindly permitted us to examine these tablets and take photographs of them. These tablets were obtained from the missionaries who had been stationed on Easter Island, and they ranged in size from 5 1/2 inches in length by 4 inches broad, to 5 1/2 feet in length and 7 inches wide. Diligent search was made for specimens of these tablets during our visit to Easter Island. At first the natives denied having any, but Mr. Salmon knew of the existence of two, and these were finally purchased after a great deal of trouble and at considerable expense. The tablets obtained are in a fair state of preservation. The large one is a piece of drift-wood that from its peculiar shape is supposed to have been used as a portion of a canoe. The other is made of the toromiro wood indigenous to the island. In explanation of the disappearance of these tablets, the natives stated that the missionaries had ordered all that could be found to be burned, with a view to destroying the ancient records, and getting rid of everything that would have a tendency to attach them to their heathenism, and prevent their thorough conversion to Christianity. The loss to the science of philology by this destruction of valuable relics is too great to be estimated. The native traditions in regard to the incised tablets simply assert that Hotu-Matua, the first king, possessed the knowledge of this written language, and brought with him to the island sixty-seven tablets containing allegories, traditions, genealogical tables, and proverbs relating to the land from which he had migrated. A knowledge of the written characters was confined to the royal family, the chiefs of the six districts into which the island was divided, sons of those chiefs, and certain priests or teachers, but the people were assembled at Anakena Bay once each year to hear all of the tablets read. The feast of the tablets was regarded as their most important fete day, and not even war was allowed to interfere with it.

The combination of circumstances that caused the sudden arrest of image-making, and resulted in the abandonment of all such work on the island, never to be again revived, may have had its effect upon the art of writing. The tablets that have been found in the best stage of preservation would correspond very nearly with the age of the unfinished images in the workshops. The ability to read the characters may have continued until 1864, when the Peruvian slavers captured a large number of the inhabitants, and among those kidnapped, were all of the officials and persons in authority. After this outrage, the traditions, etc., embraced by the tablets, seem to have been repeated on particular occasions, but the value of the characters was not understood and was lost to the natives. A man called Ure Vaeiko, one of the patriarchs of the island, professes to have been under instructions in the art of hieroglyphic reading at the time of the Peruvian visit, and claims to understand most of the characters. Negotiations were opened with him for a translation of the two tablets purchased; but he declined to furnish any information, on the ground that it had been forbidden by the priests. Presents of money and valuables were sent him from time to time, but he invariably replied to all overtures that he was now old and feeble and had but a short time to live, and declined most positively to ruin his chances for salvation by doing what his Christian instructors had forbidden. Finally the old fellow, to avoid temptation, took to the hills with the determination to remain in hiding until after the departure of the *Mohican*. It was a matter of the utmost importance that the subject should be thoroughly investigated before leaving the island, and unscrupulous strategy was the only resource after fair means had failed. Just before sundown one evening, shortly before the day appointed for our sailing, heavy clouds rolled up from the southwest and indications pointed to bad weather. In a heavy down-pour of rain we crossed the island from Vinapu to Mataveri with Mr. Salmon and found, as had been expected, that old Ure Vaeiko had sought the shelter of his own home on this rough night. He was asleep when we entered and took charge of the establishment. When he found escape impossible he became sullen, and refused to look at or touch a tablet. As a compromise it was proposed that he should relate some of the ancient traditions. This was readily acceded to, because the opportunity of relating the legends to an interested audience did not often occur, and the positive pleasure to be derived from such an occasion could not be neglected. During the recital certain stimulants that had been provided for such an emergency were produced, and though not pressed upon our ancient friend, were kept prominently before him until, as the night grew old and the narrator weary, he was included as the "cup that cheers" made its occasional rounds. A judicious indulgence in present comforts dispelled all fears in regard to the future state, and at an auspicious moment the photographs of the tablets owned by the bishop were produced for inspection. Old Ure Vaeiko had never seen a photograph before, and was surprised to find how faithfully they reproduced the tablets which he had known in his young days. A tablet would have met with opposition, but no objection could be urged against a photograph, especially something possessed by the good bishop, whom he had been instructed to reverence. The photographs were recognized immediately, and the appropriate legend related with fluency and without hesitation from beginning to end. The story of all the tablets of which we had a knowledge was finally obtained, the words of the native being written down by Mr. Salmon as they were uttered, and afterwards translated into English.

A casual glance at the Easter Island tablets is sufficient to note the fact that they differ materially from other kyriologic writings. The pictorial symbols are engraved in regular lines on depressed channels, separated by slight ridges intended to protect the heiroglyphics from injury by rubbing. In some cases the characters are smaller, and the tablets contain a greater number of lines, but in all cases the hieroglyphics are incised and cover both sides as well as the beveled edges and hollows of the board upon which they are engraved. The symbols on each line are alternately reversed; those on the first stand upright, and those on the next line are upside down, and so on by regular alternation.

This unique plan makes it necessary for the reader to turn the tablet and change its position at the end of every line; by this means the characters will be found to follow in regular procession.

The reading should commence at the lower left-hand corner, on the particular side that will bring the figures erect, and followed as the characters face in the procession, turning the tablet at the end of each line, as indicated. Arriving at the top of the first face, the reading is continued over the edge to the nearest line, at the top of the other side, and the descent continues in the same manner until the end is reached. The Boustrophedon method is supposed to have been adopted in order to avoid the possibility of missing a line of hieroglyphics.

Ure Vaeiko's fluent interpretation of the tablet was not interrupted, though it became evident that he was not actually reading the characters. It was noticed that the shifting of position did not accord with the number of symbols on the lines, and afterwards when the photograph of another tablet was substituted, the same story was continued without the change being discovered. The old fellow was quite discomposed when charged with fraud at the close of an all-night session, and at first maintained that the characters were all understood, but he could not give the signification of hieroglyphics copied indiscriminately from tablets already marked. He explained at great length that the actual value and significance of the symbols had been forgotten, but the tablets were recognized by unmistakable features and the interpretation of them was beyond question; just as a person might recognize a book in a foreign language and be perfectly sure of the contents without being able to actually read it.

Beyond doubt certain legends are ascribed to particular tablets, all of which are named, and a reference to those names will recall the appropriate story from those who do not profess to understand the hieroglyphics. An old man called Kaitae, who claims relationship to the last king, Maurata, afterwards recognized several of the tablets from the photographs and related the same story exactly as that given previously by Ure Vaeiko.

The writing is composed of pictorial symbols carrying their signification in the image they represent. The execution would be a creditable production with the assistance of the best etching tools, and is a truly wonderful result of patience and industry to be accomplished by means of obsidian points. The minute size of the hieroglyphics made it impossible to convey anything more than the general appearance of the objects delineated, but the figures may be recognized by their form in the outline drawing after the manner of some of the Egyptian hieroglyphics. The study of the tablets is chiefly difficult on account of the way in which actual objects are conventionally treated, and in order to preserve symmetry and effect, men, canoes, fish, etc., are represented of the same size throughout the lines.

A careful study of the hieroglyphics of Easter Island is being made with the hope that valuable information may be obtained in regard to the early history and origin of the people. Results of an extremely interesting nature are barely outlined at present and not in shape to be presented herewith. It is not considered expedient to attempt an explanation of the symbols until the subject can be treated exhaustively. As an example of the ideographic character of the signs, the tablet containing the genealogical tables shows a frequent repetition of the symbol of the great spirit Meke-Meke in connection with that of the female vulva. The signification is the birth of a person. The position of the figures shows whether the child was the result of marriage, or intrigue, and the following figures indicate the date of the birth, the seasons and the approximate time. An important feature, in connection with the tablets, is the fact that forms have been discovered which have no types on Easter Island, and which may lead to an identification of the locality from whence the first settlers migrated. The hieroglyphics include, besides the representation of actual objects, figures used by the chiefs, and each clan had its distinctive mark. Samples are given in different treaties made with the islanders of the sign manual of some of the chiefs.

VIII

ONE TOO HURRIED WEEK

Our pilot on our flight to the island in January of 1969 was General Paragué of the Chilean Air Force. General Paragué (pronounced Parawhey) was the man who inaugurated air traffic between Easter Island and the mainland by flying in a Catalina in 1951. He was a small modest man with a winning smile. "At that I had to crash-land," he told us in his excellent air force English. "I was never proud of that one."

He had helped lay out the airstrip and ever since had felt a paternal interest in the island and especially its flying field. He circled before he landed, to make sure, as someone suggested, there weren't any cows on the strip.

The first full view of the island seen from above gave us the impression of a small Sicily only with a volcano on each corner. The stewardesses noticed that there was not the usual welcoming throng as Paragué came in for a gentle landing. "They are all at Hangaroa trading with the French."

After a little while organizing our possessions in the green tents of the tourist colony, the bell rang for lunch. Lunch featured an excellent local crawfish. Afterwards the group of about twenty tourists collected around the pickups which were furnished with benches on the sides and we set off for our first tour of the island.

The outskirts of Hangaroa had a pleasant rustic look. As we approached the beach and the landing place on Cook's Bay everybody we passed was looking up into the sky. As we jounced out of Hangaroa the noise of helicopters became more and more deafening.

Force de Frappe

The most completely restored statue on Easter Island is at a place called Tahai. The restored monolith stands on a low headland, a piece of sculpture that takes a lot of looking at.

We found Tahai a madhouse; it was swarming with French. The sky was a pandemonium of French helicopters. The hills were full of little French sailors with red pompoms on their caps riding desperately about on the skinny island ponies.

Already, jouncing in the pickup trucks through the village of Hangaroa we'd seen gatherings of islanders staring distractedly up at the sky; they had never seen helicopters before and certainly they had never seen so many French sailors at one time. The sailors and the helicopters came off the flattop *Jeanne d'Arc* which, with its escort cruiser, was anchored off the village in what is still known as Cook's Bay in honor of Captain Cook's visit in 1774. Cadets on a training cruise, we were told. The French were showing their colors.

When, trailing after our archaeologist (Dr. Carlyle S. Smith) we tourists tried to examine the fine stonework of the platform and the statue which, with the help of a powerful crane and some contributions from *Paris-Match*, was set up several months ago with its red topknot well balanced on top of its head, a French officer, with that tact for which his nation has become famous, summarily ordered us off. He was in a hurry to take a photograph. Indeed, a group of sailors and petty officers were gathering in front of the platform all ready to say cheese while three photographers converged on them with their tripods. The tourists allowed themselves to melt into the surrounding lava slopes.

The French, though they didn't need to be so rude about it, did have a point. It was the French magazine *Paris-Match* that furnished most of the funds to reerect this particular statue when a team of their writers and photographers made a rapportage of the island in March of 1968. The venture was made painfully memorable by the fact that the two photographers were killed in an airplane crash on their way home.

The French established a relationship with Easter Island in the nineteenth century. French missionaries were the first to try to convert the natives to Christianity. In the present century it was a French ethnologist, Alfred Métraux, along with a Belgian archaeologist named Lavachery, who made the most extended study of the island before the arrival of Thor Heyerdahl's Norwegian expedition in 1955.

When we finally got back to Tahai, sailors and helicopters had gone. The warships had slipped out to sea. There was no sound but the roar of the surf. A sicklylooking cow was stumbling over the rocks to seaward of the platform and a gaunt gray horse that looked as if it had come out of Dürer's engraving of the Four Horsemen stood silhouetted against the sky on a rocky hill behind. The enormous figure with its masklike face and longlobed ears loomed solitary above our heads.

This is the only statue on the island that has its topknot. You can see what the sculptors were aiming for. The red stone of the cylinder contrasts with the brownish volcanic tuff of the monolith. The delicate balancing of great weights, cylinder on spoonshaped head, massive torso on rather slight pedestal, gives a certain exhilaration to the ensemble. We were told that in the halcyon days white coralheads were piled on the topknot as an added attraction.

Like all of them the figure faces inland. The evenly placed rounded stones of the paved court which it faced have been restored. Presumably the priest and elders performed their ceremonies on the platform while the people below faced the blue horizon and the roaring surf. The local name for the platforms is *ahu* and for the statues *moai*. A little to the left of the ahu we found the remains of a paved causeway leading down to the rocks.

There are a number of these inclined causeways. They seem to have been built to haul boats up on. They gave some imaginative visitors the idea that they were remnants of roads which led down into the civilized continent of Mu, lost in some great subsidence of land under the ocean.

Everything about Easter Island is surprising. You arrive expecting the terrain to look very ancient but geologically at least the island is comparatively recent. The beetling hills themselves are new, geologically speaking. According to the geologists the island was raised above the sea by volcanic action, bursting out of some fold of the great submerged mountain chain known as the East Pacific Ridge. The latest volcanic activity might have taken place as recently as a thousand and certainly not earlier than two or three thousand years ago. Dr. Peter Baker, the Oxford geologist who made a survey in 1966, remarked that further volcanic activity was highly likely, but refused to commit himself as to where or when an eruption might occur. This youthfulness of the land sets a limit to the period of human occupation.

The earliest carbon 14 date upon which archaeologists are generally agreed is A.D. 857. This firm date, along with the fact that no tradition of volcanic action was picked up by any of the early European visitors, would tend to place the first colonization somewhere in the seven or eight hundreds of our era. What the archaeologists call the "classical period" of statue building, which produced the conventionalized monolithic carvings, probably extended from the twelfth or thirteenth centuries into the seventeenth.

This raises an interesting and as yet unanswered question. How did an intricate stoneage culture come to flower so late on this tiny remote and inhospitable island? The stoneage cultures of Europe and Asia, of the type known to archaeologists as megalithic, date back into the second millennium of the pre-Christian era. The erection of Stonehenge is now pretty well set at between sixteen and eighteen hundred B.C.

Centuries before the first colonization of Easter Island, the people of the Chinese and Malayan coasts, thought by some historians to be the takeoff point for the Polynesian migrations into the Pacific islands, had advanced far into the bronze age. Most of them had the use of the wheel. The only highly developed stoneage civilizations during these years, whose people were ignorant of the invention of the wheel, were the civilizations of the Andean region and of Mexico and Central America.

Thor Heyerdahl, the enterprising Norwegian of *Kon-Tiki* and *Aku-Aku* fame, has devoted his life to proving that at least one early group of Easter Island settlers came on rafts or totora reed boats from the Peruvian mainland. He has the later Polynesian colonizers coming down through Hawaii from Alaska and the American Northwest Coast. The older experts on Polynesia claim that none of this could have happened. They cling to the Marquesas as the center from which the navigators in their double canoes spread over the Pacific. We still don't know who will win the debate. About all an ignorant layman can do, as he jounces in an open pickup over the rolling volcanic stones of the island's incredibly dusty roads, is, taking the arguments of the experts with a grain of salt, to try to jot down what he sees.

Vinapu

The finest megalithic masonry is at Ahu Vinapu.

The drive to Vinapu begins along a straight road through cornfields and watermelon patches past the airstrip. The same handsome brindled hawks we saw in the valleys around Santiago on the Chilean mainland soar overhead. Did somebody bring in a pair on a ship or did some persistent east wind carry them across the twenty-three hundred miles of ocean it took us nine hours to cover in a fourmotor plane? Easter Island is a place of many questions and few answers.

Instead of fences many of the fields are protected by rows of oildrums from the cattle and horses that run wild over the bare hills. Evidently the oildrums kept arriving and nobody took them away. The islanders decided to put them to use. The road, now a trail from which heavy red dust swirls about the open pickups, skirts the slopes of Rano Kao, the westernmost volcanic crater. Farther up, where the slope is steeper, the red soil shows through where a century of overgrazing by the sheepherding concerns has destroyed the vegetation.

The minute you step out of the truck you notice that the ground is strewn with shining fragments of obsidian. Obsidian, black volcanic glass, was the chief cutting tool of the islanders up to modern times; spear and javelin heads, knives and scrapers of all sorts were made of it. The bow was unknown so they needed no arrowheads. Obsidian fragments lie thick over the island as tin cans on a city dump in the States.

The Vinapu ceremonial centers—there were several of them—stand on a height overlooking the sea. Members of the Norwegian expedition found traces of a ramp that had once led up the cliff from a sheltered landing place among the rocks. According to an island tradition this was where the second group of immigrants landed, coming in canoes from the distant island of Rapa Iti southwest of the Tahitian group. Hence the modern name Rapa Nui, "Great Rapa." Rapa Iti was "Little Rapa." This was long after the arrival of the first king, Hotu Matua, who, so one story goes, leaving a "dry parched land" known as "the burial place" where he had been defeated in battle, found Easter Island by steering into the setting sun. What better description of the arid Peruvian coast could there be than "a parched land known as the burial place"?

The most impressive sight at Vinapu is the stone facing of what seems to have been the earliest platform. It is faced with beautifully squared volcanic stones that must weigh several tons each, fitted together with extraordinary delicacy. This is the ahu that reminded Heyerdahl of the stonework at Tiahuanaco in the Bolivian highlands near Lake Titicaca.

Standing beside it on the dry grassy slope facing the Pacific, which rings the island with a roaring barrier of surf, I couldn't help remembering running my fingers, a few years ago in the high Andes, along the neat joints of the megalithic walls round the ancient Peruvian capital at Cuzco.

The indefatigable Paymaster Thomson was so intrigued with this structure that he blew up a piece of the wall with gunpowder to see how it was constructed inside. A casual visitor can't help being struck by the fact that wherever he goes on Easter Island it is the earliest masonry that shows the most skillful workmanship.

One of the chief aims of the Norwegian expedition was to establish firm dates by carbon 14 analysis. These analyses proved somewhat disappointing. It took a lot of discussion for the archaeologists to agree on A.D. 857 (plus or minus two hundred years) as the earliest date found on the island. This was obtained from ashes dug out from under the earth mound round the court of what seems the second most ancient ahu at Vinapu. They are still vague as to whether that date should represent the beginning or the end of the building there.

There is now a method of dating by measuring the disintegration of obsidian. This has already been used to check some of the erratic results of carbon dating. In the future it should be particularly helpful in the establishment of an Easter Island chronology, since obsidian appears to be in abundance in all but the earliest strata investigated.

The erection of these ceremonial centers in the megalithic style is reckoned to have covered a period of some 250 years. What sculptured figures there were seem to have been set within the courts. It is likely that they were far more realistic than the later "classical" monoliths. Everything you see on Easter Island brings up questions. Why should the structure assigned the earliest date exhibit the greatest refinement of stoneage technique? It would seem a safe guess that the stonemasons learned their skills somewhere else.

It must have taken generations of trial and error to develop the techniques needed for the erection of the megalithic walls. Picture the intelligently directed teamwork which went into splitting these huge chunks off from the quarry, squaring them with basalt picks, hauling them on rollers or sledges over rough terrain for many miles, and then fitting them with perfect precision into place. Hundreds of men must have worked for months on each operation. They had to be fed and furnished with water. The more they learn about the constructions of the stoneage peoples, the more archaeologists are astonished by the teamwork that accomplished it. Hundreds and thousands of men were organized to a single purpose. We are beginning to think of the coordination of brain and muscle needed to create these megalithic structures as comparable in human effort to the organization that goes into rocket launchings in our day.

In the early period these ceremonial buildings contained courts enclosed by earth embankments. The ahus were always on the ocean side. If statues were set up they were within the court, probably in the style of the crouched bearded figure Heyerdahl dug up near the main quarry at Rano Raraku which reminded him of statues he had seen in the ruins of Tiahuanaco in the Bolivian highlands.

The earliest ahus were carefully oriented to the equinoctial sun or the solstices. Their builders prized their knowledge of astronomy. Some ahus show signs of having been abandoned for a period of years and then repaired with smaller but still carefully matched stones. By this time the builders had forgotten the earlier people's interest in solar observation. What is known as the "classical period" of stone carving had begun.

Wherever the early techniques of setting squared stone were developed, there is no question that the moais or monolithic statues that crowd Easter Island were a native invention. Most of the ahus of the first period were rebuilt to form pedestals for them. There is nothing quite like them in the world.

The Birdmen

The best gravel road on the island leads up the easterly slope of the crater of Rano Kao to a spot near the rim. Turning back as you climb down from the truck you get your first good view of the island. It forms a triangle with a volcano at each corner. Across the island from Rano Kao the heights of Rano Aroi today are veiled in rain. Beyond are the uneasy hills that hide the quarry crater of Rano Raraku and the coneshaped eminence ending in a great cliff that caps the Poike peninsula at the eastern end.

As you walk into the wind along the narrow path that follows the crater's rim you find yourself looking down eight hundred feet into the cauldron. In the bottom a quaking bog masks a lake of considerable depth. Around its banks grows the totora reed that gave Heyerdahl one of his most cogent arguments in support of his theory of the American origin of the Easter Island culture.

Totora is supposed to grow nowhere else in the Pacific, but it is plentiful on Lake Titicaca and around irrigated land on the Peruvian coast, where it was used in pre-Incaic times to build boats and the one-man floats used for fishing. These more or less conical floats made of bundled reeds lashed together were used by the Easter Islanders as late as the early years of the present century.

Drills were used on the crater floor by members of the Norwegian expedition to obtain cores for a pollen count. From these cores it appears that the island was at one time heavily forested. More than twenty varieties of trees grew there. The totora reed appeared suddenly after a period of burning. Unluckily no date seems to have been established for its introduction.

The inner slope of the cauldron is very steep. In times of drought, even in recent years women have been known to climb the long slope up from Hangaroa and down into the crater carring gourds to fetch water for their households. The crater was inhabited in early times. Traces of housefoundations and terraced croplands can still be seen towards the bottom of the inner slope. Among the abundant vegetation growing there is said to be the last survivor of the *toromiro*, an aboriginal tree very important to the island's economy in the old days.

The western rim of the crater opposite from where we stand is a knifeedge. Erosion from the pounding waves continually eats away the lava on the ocean side. It is thought that trying to ride around that part of the rim was how a promising young Chilean geologist lost his life a few months back. It is likely that the horse slipped on the narrow edge. Horse and man must have plunged a thousand feet into the sea. No trace was ever found of either horse or rider or of his geologist's equipment. The latest of Easter Island's many unsolved mysteries.

The ceremonial village of Orongo which you stumble on suddenly along the narrow footpath is one of the most romantic spots on the face of the earth. On one side is the deep cauldron of the crater, on the other the cliff. There's a dizzy sense of height.

The constructions occupy a wedgeshaped flattening of the crater rim. The rocks that bound the ceremonial platforms hang over an enormous expanse of azure ocean and the three islets where the islanders collected seabirds' eggs. The surf is heavy today. The pointed rocks stand up out of a marbled white and green spume of broken waves.

The low stone structures are roofed with stone slabs. Some of them have entrances through the roof which give them somewhat the air of the ceremonial chambers in the pueblos of our Southwest. A number of holes bored into virgin rock were discovered by the Norwegians to constitute a solar observation station. On December 22, the summer solstice, a pole thrust at sunrise into the largest hole casts a shadow right across one of the smaller holes. At equinox the shadow covers another hole and so on around the sun's four stages which establish the seasons of the year. A great deal more knowledge than is obvious at first glance must have gone into the setting up of this simple contraption.

As you pick your way among the tumbled rocks with the seawind in your face you begin to notice that every bowlder is carved. The volcanic rock swarms with figures in low relief. First thing you make out is the goggleeyed mask of Makemake, whom the islanders considered the basic divinity whose power underlay all the phenomena of earth and sky.

There's an electric energy about the carving of the birdmen. In topsy-turvy juxtaposition you can make out a swarm of human figures with birds' heads, long hands raised in supplication.

Some of the heads seem to be of frigatebirds; there is a hawk-like curve to their beaks. Others have straight beaks like the sooty tern. It has been suggested that at some period the sooty tern was more abundant on the nesting islands and at another the frigate-bird. The emotional intensity of these carvings testifies to how much the islanders needed seabirds' eggs.

Their diet was deficient in many ways. The only meat was the longlegged Polynesian chicken—said by the way to have laid blue eggs—and a ratlike creature, now extinct. Pigs and the Maori dogs fattened for eating, which were a staple in most Polynesian lands, never reached Easter Island. Fish and turtles, said to have been abundant in early times, fell into short supply as skills diminished and as trees large enough to fashion canoes out of became unobtainable. They did have rock lobsters and shellfish.

The list of the foods they lacked is formidable. They had neither beans, rice, wheat nor corn. Breadfruit wouldn't grow. There had been coconut palms but they died out. Their food crops were bananas, sugarcane, many varieties of sweet potatoes, a few yams and a limited amount of taro. Chilipeppers, a small tomato and wild pineapples might possibly be added to the list.

It is easy to understand that the yearly arrival of the seabirds and the harvest of eggs that followed was an event of paramount importance.

The bird cult at Orongo seems to have been one of the earliest established and one of the last to lapse. Though excavation yielded no carbon 14 dates earlier than the fifteenth century, the stonework of certain constructions made the archaeologists pretty sure that the cult existed there hundreds of years earlier. The latest date yielded by the ashes of ceremonial fires was 1857 and reports have drifted down of ceremonies as late as 1867.

Many descriptions of the ceremonies have come down. Sometime during the winter months the tribes gathered at Mataveri near the site of the present airstrip. Then after a season of games and festivals the chief men climbed up Rano Kao and took up their abode in the ceremonial shelters. In the eighteenth and nineteenth centuries only the dominant tribes shared this privilege. While their wise men chanted legends from the rongo-rongo tablets men and women performed dances and fertility rites. At the sight of the first arriving seabirds the tribal chiefs—or later their representatives known as *hopu*—climbed down the cliff and swam across to the islands in full sight below. They may have used hornshaped one-man floats of totora reed but according to tradition many drowned on the way. The first man to find a bird's egg shouted up to the elders watching on the high cliff above and, with the egg in his mouth, swam back through the breakers and climbed the heights to the ceremonial platform.

The chief who through his own prowess or that of his hopu captured the first egg became the birdman of the year. His head was shaved and he was painted with special designs. He lived in seclusion surrounded by taboos. His followers are said to have expressed their satisfaction by raiding and plundering the defeated tribes whose chiefs had failed in the contest.

It was in 1868 that H.M.S. *Topaze* visited the island and carried off from Orongo the basalt statue, probably an example of the earliest style of the classical period, which so impressed my childish imagination when I first saw it in the British Museum. Mr. J. L. Palmer, surgeon aboard, wrote a careful report on the ceremonial village. On the walls of the cavelike shelters he found modern paintings of European-style ships superimposed on the engravings of what are now supposed to be early ships made of lashedtogether bundles of totora reed. He discovered the statue partly buried, still revered by the islanders as Hoa-kaka-nana-ia, the Breaker of the Waters. With the help of some natives and three hundred sweating British tars Palmer managed to get it transported down the mountain and aboard ship and carried it off to England.

The statue's name and the ships on the surrounding petroglyphs and a series of traditions recorded in the early part of this century have given some archaeologists the idea that a cult of ships, handed down from the times when navigation was a fact instead of a dim memory, was associated with the birdman cult at Orongo.

The disappearance of the statue, combined with the conversion of the Pascuenses to Christianity, put an end to the ceremonies.

Rano Raraku

Rano Raraku contained the great central quarries where the "classical style" statues were created. The name is said to mean crater with a passageway. The passageway is a deep cutting excavated through the rim in early times to make it easier to haul out statues carved in the quarries on the inner slope. As at Rano Kao, a lake occupies the crater bowl but this one is shallow. It is thickly grown with totora reed higher than your head. Today blue water shimmers through the green reeds under a sunny sky.

Inside and out this crater represents a most extraordinary gallery of sculpture. Some twenty erect statues in various stages of completion rise in tiers on the inner slope towards the dark rim-rock above. As many more have fallen or lie unfinished in the quarries.

The outer slope fairly bristles with them. About fifty still stand where they were set, either as sentinels for the busy quarries or awaiting transportation to some ahu by the shore. Many of them have been buried up to the neck by slides down the steep cone. A good twenty lie flat on their faces along trails at the volcano's base as if abandoned en route to their destination. Members of the Norwegian expedition were convinced that many more lay buried under the vast piles of rubble that resulted from centuries of work in the quarries. Some 160 are still attached to the virgin

tuff in various stages of manufacture. Carbon dates from A.D.
1206 (plus or minus a hundred years) were recorded from excavations round the statues' bases.

The landscape somehow fits the titanic quality of the works
of man. Wan grasses cover the wide empty plain that stretches
from the nearby coast as far as you can see to the northward. No
sheep, no horses, no cattle. Even the hawks seem to shun this
end of the island. To the east rise the shadowy hills grouped
around the easternmost headland on the Poike peninsula. To the
south the infinite Pacific stretches to the horizon.

The statues, with masklike heads and torsos ending in the carefully delineated breechclout which forms a base, all follow a conventional design, but different stages of erosion and the variations
of sun and shadow give them different expressions. On some the
lips pout with arrogance, on others the deep eyesockets express
a heartbroken melancholy. Some of the long lobes of the perforated ears show a trace of ornamental plugs, others not. The
noses vary a great deal. Some of the nostrils are more or less
naturalistic, others conventionalized. The sculptors developed a
variety of ways of expressing the details of breast and navel.

Their sheer immensity is overwhelming. The largest standing
on the slope measures more than thirty-seven feet and is reckoned
to weigh sixty-four tons. An unfinished giant still attached to
the quarry wall measures eight-two feet.

After you get used to the size you find yourself examining the
monoliths as pieces of sculpture. Wherever you catch a glimpse
of an unweathered surface you are surprised by the delicacy of
the finish. These were not the roughhewn figures they appear
after centuries of weathering. They vary immensely in workmanship, but the best of them, once you grant the sculptors their
peculiar conventions, are works of art of a very high order. The
seven statues in a row William Mulloy restored to their ahu at
Akivi, though they lack the topknots that completed the design,
give an idea of the eerie superhuman impressiveness the sculptors
aimed for.

What did they represent to their sculptors? It is possible that
like the totem poles of the Northwest Indians they represented
divine ancestors and family heroes? As in most European
sculpture of the last decades, realism is sacrificed for emotional

and symbolic impact; and in this case to ceremonial fitness. But these sculptors never lost the humanity of their figures. The impression is of people, sad distant perhaps superhuman people, but people. You have to examine some part of the surface which has been protected from the weather to appreciate the high finish the carvings originally had. Their present roughhewn look is the result of the erosion of the volcanic tuff they are carved out of by centuries of wind and rain. Some investigators think that, like the Greek marbles, they were originally painted.

The finest piece of work of them all, in fact in my opinion the finest thing on Easter Island, is the buried basalt monster the Norwegians uncovered somewhat apart from the rest on the southern slope of Rano Raraku. The statue had been buried so deep that none of the islanders knew of its existence. It is thought to date from the early period before A.D. 1100. It represents a naked man squatting on his heels. The head, exaggerated in size, is tilted up as if looking into immense distances. The cheekbones are broad, the eyesockets deep. A small chinbeard gives the face an oddly aristocratic look. The quality of the carving is hardly diminished by the pitting and erosion of centuries. The people who produced this sculpture must have had long years of technical training behind them.

The Battle of Poike Ditch

The legends that have clustered about the quarries are as dramatic as the scene itself. The carving of statues seems to have gone on at an everincreasing pace through the seventeenth century. The amount of work performed was incredible. The theory is that it took a team of twenty men something like a year to carve out the hugest ones and to detach them from the quarry wall. Nobody hazards a guess as to how long the finishing and polishing took. The teams, possibly representing various clans or families as in the birdegg contest, seem to have competed more and more wildly. Something of the sort has occasionally gone on among the skyscraper builders of our great cities. A building "taller than the Empire State" is under construction right now in New York City.

Until Heyerdahl induced the Atan brothers to set a statue back on its pedestal for him at Anakena Beach, the problem of how the statues were transported was considered insoluble. The old men gravely told the missionaries that the statues walked to their pedestals. Their ancestors had the *mana*, the magic power, to accomplish such things.

Heyerdahl's crew, with the help of ropes, using long poles for leverage and pushing in stones to support the statue after each tiny hoist, managed to lift and slide a twenty-five-ton monolith into a position where its base was even with the basalt pedestal on which it originally stood. Twelve men worked ten days on this part of the operation. The then *alcalde*, Pedro Atan, whose family claimed descent from the "Longears" who embodied the ancient traditions of the island, supervised the work. His story was that an elderly relative had told him how it was done when he was a small boy. Another eight days and the job was successfully completed. The statue was back on its ahu, where it now broods over the stony slope leading down to Anakena Beach.

Asked how the figures were hauled down from the quarry, Atan built a Y-shaped sledge. With the help of 150 islanders Heyerdahl invited to a feast, he moved a ten-ton statue a considerable distance without much difficulty. From these operations, William Mulloy, the American archaeologist who seems most familiar with Easter Island problems, deduced the ingenious theory that the bigger monoliths may have been moved in a half-upright position, using the weight of the statue balanced on the curve of its belly to shift it forward with a rocking motion a few feet at a time. The statue would have been supported meanwhile by some sort of bipod hoisting gear which would have moved with each move of the statue. However the transportation was accomplished, it took infinite patience, muscle and knowhow.

Rolling the cylindrical topknots from their quarry in the center of the island offered no great problem, but getting them up on top of the statues' heads was a real feat of engineering. The supposition is that the piles of stones left over from the statues' erection were used as an inclined plane; but how the ten- or twenty-ton cylinders could have been balanced on top of the great stone heads without the use of a modern crane baffles the imagination.

The island tradition is that four roads led from the quarry, across which the statues were transported on sledges or cradles. According to one story mashed sweet potatoes were used as a lubricant. Traces of the roads have been found. Legends persist that there were once smoothly paved roads all over the island. Among the facts and fancies collected by Paymaster Thomson was the story an old man told him: Before the first settlement by the present race of islanders, a previous race had covered the island with a network of beautifully paved, treeshaded roads in the shape of a spider's web.

Somewhere around 1680 the climax of statue building was reached. After hundreds of years of everincreasing activity, a sudden catastrophe ended the statue building forever. The carvers dropped their tools and went away. Their basalt picks litter the excavations to this day.

Here the legends recited to the early missionaries and the archaeological evidence combine to fix a fairly firm date. Somewhere late in the seventeenth century a great battle was fought between two groups of islanders. The legends call them the Longears and the Shortears. The Longears commanded the sculptors and stonemasons. They may have dominated the island from very early times. Their chief men wore ornaments in the elongated lobes of their ears. From Paymaster Thomson's visit on, abundant evidence has been uncovered that two separate groups of people inhabited the island; one lived in stone houses and the other in long communal thatched dwellings shaped like overturned canoes. The Shortears, who lived in the boatshaped houses, may have been descended from immigrants who arrived from islands to the west during the period of the great Polynesian voyages in the thirteenth century.

According to the legends the final battle was fought in a manmade depression, known as the Poike ditch, that cuts off the eastern peninsula with its thousand-foot volcanic cone. The story was told that the Longears built the ditch for defense and filled it with brush, intending to burn up the Shortears in it, but the Shortears overwhelmed them and destroyed them to the last man.

Recent diggings confirm the story so far as a conflagration

is concerned; but the ditch, instead of a fortification, seems to have been a long sunken garden where bananas and sugarcane and taro were grown sheltered from the heavy winds that so hampered the growing of crops on the island. In a time of civil war the plantations were burned.

Wherever it took place the "battle of Poike ditch" marked the end of coordinated effort and of order and prosperity. A mania for destruction seized the islanders. They put almost as much work into pulling down the statues as they had in setting them up.

The carving and the moving and the erection of these strange effigies must have absorbed the energies of hundreds if not thousands of men, over a long period. Teamwork on that scale could only have been possible in a time of peace and plenty. The scanty resources of the island must have been developed to their utmost. That meant a harmonious and efficient social system.

Somehow the system cracked. Civil war broke out. Here the carbon dating corresponds to the date Father Sebastian Englert deduced from genealogies recited to him by old men who remembered the times before the slave raids and the smallpox. Father Sebastian set the date as 1670. The radiocarbon date, taken from the ashes of the conflagration that destroyed the plantations in the Poike ditch, was, give or take a hundred years, 1668.

To this day the casual visitor sees evidence of a sudden overturn with his own eyes. Statues in the quarries were abandoned half-finished. The carvers dropped their basalt picks and moved away. Statues en route to their locations by the seashore still lie abandoned where they fell.

The legends agree that at some point the Shortears rose up against the Longears. These were people who stretched the lobes of their ears with ornamental earplugs. One can't help thinking of the *Orejónes* whose long ears astonished Pizarro at the court of the Incas. They were the guardians of tradition and the interpreters of the written language brought in on wooden tablets by Hotu Matua, who, though the stories conflict as to whether he came from the east or the west, was universally revered as the first king and culture hero. The pretext for the uprising according to one tale was that the Longears ordered the Shortears to pick up all the stones on the island and throw them into the sea.

Suddenly all the carefully developed skills were turned to the purposes of destruction. At ahus such as Akivi you can see where the statues were toppled in a row. "What good are they?" you can almost hear the people saying. "Let's pull them down." You can almost see the wreckers, hauling with ropes and prying with poles, pulling them down one after another. A certain awe seems to have clung to them. Over some of them they piled pyramidal cairns. The abandoned ahus, still considered holy ground, became burial places.

The early Christian missionaries found it hard to get any work out of the Easter Islanders. They all remarked on this destructive mania, which they considered part of their devilish paganism. The wrecking continued intermittently for a couple of hundred years.

Continual wars destroyed the economy. Teamwork went by the board. It was only with first-rate organization that the island had been able to support a population which could hardly have amounted to more than five or six thousand in the most prosperous times.

The resources were limited indeed. The destruction of the sunken gardens, which must have been cultivated with extreme care, meant disaster.

The clans and families took to raiding each other for slaves. Cannibalism for food became an established practice. No man's life was safe. Almost every house on the island was burned or pulled down. Even the foundation curbings were uprooted. Families took refuge in caves. At the same time, though wood-carving survived, the people forgot most of their crafts. Though pollen counts prove the island to have been heavily wooded at some early age, few trees were now left with large enough trunks to make canoes. The art of building the ships of totora reed that are illustrated in some of the petroglyphs had already lapsed. By the time the first Europeans arrived the tribes were living in a state of anarchy amid the ruins of their past civilization.

As archaeological work enables us to learn more details about the life of the Easter Islanders the place may get to be thought of as a sort of laboratory for the study of why men act as they do. Though there are immense cultural and racial differences, certain broad outlines of human behavior seem unchanged since the earliest records. Here you have a small group of people living for several centuries in comparative isolation, developing very special accomplishments in stonework and carving, and then forgetting almost all their skills in an orgy of destructiveness.

Even with the limited information we have today, seen on the spot the story becomes extraordinarily dramatic. During a period of peace and plenty the islanders had enough leisure, after their fishing and farming had satisfied their food requirements, to put an immense amount of energy into the erection of the monuments that litter the volcanoes today.

Up in the quarries you can crawl around the unfinished sculptures, you can feel the contours of the carefully worked stone. You can handle the basalt picks that were the sculptors' chief tools. You can't help feeling that this skillful artistic and engineering work must have given the islanders a happy feeling of accomplishment. Setting up great statues might not seem important to present-day Americans but to these people it must have been the be-all and the end-all.

Then suddenly, so far as we know without any foreign invasion, all this energy was turned towards destruction. With the release from statue building the whole carefully balanced social order which had afforded the islanders a fairly comfortable and satisfactory life collapsed too. Famine and warfare took its place.

Twenty years ago, even ten years ago, the Easter Island story wouldn't have seemed so cogent to an American. We were still hopefully committed to the building of a civilization. It never occurred to us that we were breeding a generation of wreckers. Great blocks of steel and glass skyscrapers full of the whir of typewriters and people pushing papers back and forth across desks probably wouldn't have seemed any more important to an Easter Islander than their weird statues seem to us, but we see them as part of a complicated social structure which assures food, clothing and shelter and an incredible number of amenities to many millions of people. Today, again without any massive impulse from the outside, counterparts have appeared in our society of the wreckers who had themselves a time pulling down the silly old statues on Easter Island. "None of it is any good, let's make an end of it."

Probably it didn't occur to the Easter Island revolutionists any more than it does to our college radicals that their own food and shelter depended on the social order they were pulling down. Undoubtedly agitators told them that if they overthrew the statues the oppression of the Longears would fall with them. Justice and plenty would reign. Nobody would have to work any more. The result was a hundred years of arson and famine and murder and the near extinction of a talented and effective community.

Every human group that has accomplished anything leaves behind a lesson for posterity. If we could learn these lessons in time we might find ways to avoid our own destruction. The more we study the record that vanished cultures have left behind them the clearer it becomes that man's capacity for creative work is almost infinite, but that it is matched almost evenly by the impulse to destroy.

The nineteenth century was a black time for the Easter Islanders. As contacts with Europeans increased their society became more and more demoralized. Syphilis and TB did their work. Every man's hand was against his brother. The rage for destruction was unabated. The last of the great monoliths on an ahu on the north shore was pulled down as late as 1860.

Two years later came the Peruvian slave raids that meant the end of what was left of the island's culture. Nine hundred or so of the inhabitants were carried off to work on the guano islands. Among them, so the story goes, were all the *maori*, the leading men, who had been educated to read the rongo-rongo tablets. Many of them died. When the survivors were repatriated, as the result of a vigorous protest by Bishop Jaussen of Tahiti and by the French ambassador to Peru, they brought smallpox back with them. By the time the French missionaries were established on the island in the middle eighteen sixties the population had been reduced, according to one account, to 111 souls.

Brother Eugène Eyraud, a dedicated man who gave up a good business as a machinist in Chile to preach the gospel to these poor heathen, had rough going. The Pascuenses took everything he had and finally drove him off the island. "The mission," wrote Father Pacôme Olivier, "is being established at a time when the destructive work has reached its extreme limits, destruction of both material and moral kind. This island was formerly covered by a beautiful vegetation, traces of which still remain, but all has been destroyed; at present not a tree is seen. This instinct of destruction, together with theft, seems to be the dominant characteristic of the people. . . ."

IX

THE RONGO-RONGO TABLETS

The chief enigma in connection with Easter Island remains the system of writing, which according to tradition was brought in by Hotu Matua and his first two boatloads of settlers. The existence of wooden tablets inscribed with some sort of meaningful signs was unsuspected by Europeans until a small boy brought Father Zumbohm an inscribed plank which he was using to wind fishnets on. Since the inscriptions looked like unmistakable hieroglyphics to him, the missionary became very much interested. Brother Eugène Eyraud then began to notice that similar inscribed tablets were hanging in almost every reed hut. What surprised him most was that some of the animals depicted in the signs did not exist on the island. Father Zumbohm immediately got together several elderly men learned in the traditions of the Maori and asked them to decipher a particularly clear inscription. Each man started chanting but each said the others were wrong. Father Zumbohm could not get them to agree on any one interpretation.

When Bishop Jaussen of Tahiti got wind of the tablets he was immensely excited because he was sure that no other system of writing existed in the Polynesian world. He wrote to the missionaries to collect and preserve all they could; by the time the missionaries started looking for them most of the tablets had disappeared. The islanders were closemouthed on the subject; they thought the tablets had magical power, and being now fervent Christians, while they feared the *mana* of the tablets, they considered magic a sin. Scholars all over the world became interested. Occasionally some investigator managed to get some old man to attempt to decipher an inscription, but the result was that he chanted some legend he thought to be connected with the particular tablet he was confronted with. The islanders were certain that the rongo-rongo were the repositories of the genealogies and histories of their ancestors but the signs themselves remained impenetrable.

Efforts to match the signs with the sounds and words of the Polynesian dialect now spoken on the island have ended in confusion. Between 1864 and Brother Eyraud's death in 1868 every tablet he had seen vanished. The Pascuenses seem to have hidden them in the caves, where according to an old tradition, they secreted their valuables. About twenty now survive in European museums. Interpretation has been made more rather than less difficult by Heyerdahl's discovery that right up to the present the islanders are very privately trying to preserve their own version of the characters. Father Sebastian took him to see an elderly leper who was spending his last days copying out a list of characters. Later he discovered that the Atan family had a number of such manuscripts in their possession, copied out mostly in old school notebooks.

Efforts to decipher the tablets by the cryptogrammic methods so successful with the Cretan scripts have proved so far fruitless. We know exactly as much, after years of learned wrangling, as Father Zumbohm did after he'd tried to get his group of islanders to decipher the first tablets he discovered. Heyerdahl did endless research to develop his theory of a Peruvian origin not only of Easter Island writing but of the entire culture of the ahu-building period. Heyerdahl's argument was heavily reinforced by his discovery of the actual remains of the round stone huts, only accessible from the roof, which Father Sebastian's informants told him were used as schoolhouses where the boys were taught to read and write according to the rongo-rongo system. The latest finding, reported to the Moscow Anthropological Congress in

1964 by a group of Russian linguistic experts who had been analyzing the pictographs according to modern decoding methods, was that the signs must refer to a language far different from the present dialect spoken on Easter Island. The fact stands out that the reversed boustrophedon script is only found on Easter Island and in a number of systems developed in pre-Incaic Peru and the Tiahuanaco period. Recently similar systems have been found in use by some Indians of the Isthmus of Panama.

Easter Island prehistory remains a series of enigmas. Where did the masons come from who did the early stonework? Who developed the unique style of the statues of the classical period? Thor Heyerdahl's primary theory, that the earliest stoneage culture came from the Peruvian coast, though he certainly proved his point with the *Kon-Tiki,* was received with universal disapproval by professional archaeologists. To an interested layman it would still appear that he delivered some telling arguments in his *American Indians in the Pacific.* His secondary theory, that the aboriginal Polynesians entered the Pacific via Hawaii from the west coast of what is now Canada and Alaska, would seem to suffer from the fact that Polynesian is generally considered one of the Malay group of languages. However, it takes no great scholarship to deduce from the arguments pro and con that there was more navigation of the Pacific from east to west and west to east during the years of the great migrations than has generally been imagined.

A great deal of archaeological and anthropological work remains to be done before the enigmas of Easter Island prehistory can be even halfway resolved. After all it is only recently that a satisfactory sequence has been established for Mexican pre-history. Barely twenty years have gone by since brilliant young Covarrubias was derided by the archaeologists for insisting on his artist's hunch that the Olmecs represented the earliest mid-American civilization. Now, long after Covarrubias' death, careful archaeological work and repeated carbon datings at La Venta and Tres Zapotes have proved his point. I suspect that a few of Heyerdahl's heresies will eventually find similar acceptance.

X

THE PASCUENSES TODAY

Back in the winter of 1969, our amateur archaeology was interrupted by the arrival of Father Sebastian's body on a Chilean Air Force plane. His parishioners crowded around and reverently transferred the coffin to a pickup truck. It looked as if everybody on the island followed the cortege to the church. The Pascuenses sang plainsong as they walked after the coffin, many of them with tears in their eyes. I've rarely heard such heartbreaking singing. The Pascuenses sing very true, simple hymnlike songs that resound most touchingly under the bright sky.

Next day the Bishop of the Araucanians from Villarrica conducted the burial mass. He was a large man with a spadeshaped beard. His assistants, also bearded Capuchins, were large men too. One of them was blond and the other dark. The Bishop's eulogy of Father Sebastian was worthy of the man, expressed in clear-as-crystal Spanish. He spoke of Father Sebastian's modesty and self-sacrifice as Franciscan virtues. It had been particularly Father Sebastian's childlike modesty that had appealed to his parishioners, on this dismal and desolate island. No matter how much praise and how many awards he won from foreign scientific societies, for his archaeological work, he came back to his people

146

the same modest unassuming priest, a confessor who really was the father of his congregation.

Singing is the natural expression of the Pascuenses. The men and women of the congregation sang the entire burial mass, some of it in Tahitian, which is the church language because Christianity came to them through Tahiti, some in Pascuense. I even thought I heard a few words of Latin. There was no accompaniment. They lifted up their voices and sang their grief.

I never attended a burial service where such sincere grief was so beautifully expressed. It didn't sound like any mass we had ever heard. When they stopped it was the breaking of a spell.

Everybody crowded around the little graveyard where room had been made for Father Sebastian beside Brother Eyraud, the first missionary. There was so little space among a few rose bushes there was no room for more burials. The lay authorities took over with a few short speeches. The rifle corps from the Chilean Air Force fired a volley as the coffin was lowered in the grave.

Tears come easily to the Pascuenses but these two men for them had embodied everything that was best in Christianity. Their teachings were sincerely accepted. One felt sure that there was no nostalgia for the old days of superstition and robbery and cannibalism. The Pascuenses were not only accepting the Christian world. They were reaching out after it.

It is always a surprise anywhere in this world to find an attractive school building. The new school at Hangaroa was light and airy and had an unexpectedly festive look. We were invited in after dinner for the Pascuense inauguration, and were seated on benches in the large hall. A folkloric group, natives of Easter Island, started dancing and singing and that was all. It was the pleasantest school meeting we had ever seen. No speeches, none of those formal addresses with which Chilean officials had inaugurated the school earlier in the afternoon.

Efforts were made to induce the visitors to join in the hulas. It was a delightful sight to see the Minister of Education, a short stoutish man in a dark suit, trying to join in. Nobody was induced to do anything he didn't want to do. Everything was carried off lightly. Nobody's dignity was offended. The Pascuenses have that knack.

Another evening we went out to a lobster hunt. A team of guitarists played in the light of a bonfire. The firelight was mirrored in the dark and green patches of an inlet. Out there men and boys were hunting for rock lobsters with torches from under the ledges. There was quite a hurrah as various of the visitors attempted hulas. The guitars were still playing and the lobsters were still being brought in when we went off to bed.

We had been exchanging messages with Alfonso Rapu, the *alcalde*—or mayor—who was the elected representative of the local people. He was offering to show us his island. Finally after lunch one day he turned up. He was driving a pickup. Nobody but the governor drove a car.

Alfonso Rapu was a young man of great charm. He was tall with a coppery Polynesian sheen to his skin, large dark eyes and the sort of almost plump figure you see in swimming champions. In fact he confided to us that swimming was his favorite sport. He swam a mile out to sea every morning of his life. We looked at the heavy surf roaring on the rocks and marveled. "Here we are used to it . . . from the time we were little children."

He explained that the officials from the Department of Education had kept him busy. Now that the official plane was taking off he could catch his breath.

First he took us to see his uncle's new house. He felt it was remarkable that a man working alone, with only occasional help from his nephews, could have accomplished so much. The uncle was a dark thinfaced man. His face had a special bony structure. His features reminded us of the small statuettes of starving people, known as *kava kava* figures, the Pascuenses execute in such numbers for the tourist trade. We had been running into traces of this special cast of countenance throughout the island and were calling it privately "the Pascuense look."

The most perfect example was an odd youth—the spitting image of Pierre Loti's Petro—who policed the tents at "the hotel." His name was Raoul; when we asked him what he did he answered in English that he was a professional dancer. When we saw him dancing at the school festivities it was obvious that his was no empty boast. He was undoubtedly the best dancer on the island.

Alfonso's uncle's house was a pleasant stucco and cinder block affair with large windows and airy rooms, of the sort modest families are building around Santiago. He had built it with his own hands and the help of his nephews. When he said "built it himself" he really meant it, cinder block by cinder block. How he ever collected the hardware, the doors and windows, the cement and stucco one could hardly imagine. And the mayor's uncle's was not the only one of its sort going up in Hangaroa.

The chief entertainments among the Pascuenses were still dancing and singing. There was great interest in reviving the local folklore. The night we arrived the folklore group invited all the tourists to a *sau-sau* or banquet. Yams and pork were cooked in an earth oven. The entertainment was in a lovely banana grove off the road going to Hangaroa. I've always found Polynesian food pretty hard to put down. This was no exception. Much more interesting was the dancing and singing. A number of young men all of whom appeared taller than even Alfonso Rapu danced in, wearing tall conical hats of white chicken feathers which made them look high as a house. Their demeanor was almost terrifyingly stately. The girls were correspondingly feminine and fluffy in white chicken feather hula skirts.

We were tired and had to go back early to our scotch and water in the green tent, but even after we were tucked away in our cots we could feel the soft rhythms and the charming voices of the hula.

The only other art that has been handed down, especially, we were told, in certain families, is wood carving. As early as Pierre Loti's time the Pascuenses were trading wood carvings and island antiquities with passing ships. Salmon the sheepherder established quite a business sending Easter Island antiquities for sale to Tahiti. In later years the practice has grown. Heyerdahl found they were palming off recent reproductions for the real thing. The Atun family who helped him reconstruct the method of erecting and moving the great monoliths were not above tucking an occasional reproduction in with the genuine articles they turned over to him. They now have a store where they sell Easter Island antiquities in Valparaiso. We met outside of Villarrica a young Chilean *aficionado* of island folklore who had brought back two Pascuense carvers to set them up in Chile. Distance from the island did not seem to have affected their skill. They showed us some beautiful pieces they were working on. Already they were allowing themselves some slight variations of the traditional forms.

Wood carving, now that supplies of carvable wood can be obtained from the mainland, bids fair to become the chief industry of the island. The whittling is all freehand, done with extraordinary speed and freedom. One of our fellow tourists happened by a family at work. Their whole stock had gone to the French in exchange for wine earlier in the week. They sat under a tree back of their house working away while a young man played the guitar to them. They worked at top speed, drinking and singing. They were building up a backlog of *kava kava* figures for sale or trading with our batch of tourists before our plane left next day.

Alfonso Rapu took us for a drive in the country to see the two new pumping stations. He was inordinately proud of the two wells which were already at work and the third one which would come in pretty soon. It meant that for the first time in their history the Pascuenses could have enough good water. It was extremely pure water at that, discovered in deep fissures between the lava flows a couple of hundred feet down. We walked around fields of watermelon, corn, tomatoes and sweet potatoes, talking to the cultivators. As a last treat the *alcalde* drove us down to the shore. There, in a fishing shack which might have been on the coast of Maine we found a man tanned almost black. He had the massive figure of one of the basalt statues. He did little talking. Probably his Spanish was poor. But he didn't need to talk. He had two heavy-duty Swedish outboard motors in the shack and—we could hardly believe our eyes—a girl working on an adding machine.

Before we left he drew two magnificent crawfish out of a burlap bag and presented them to my wife. The *alcalde* had run out of time. He drove us fast to the mess shack where they were delighted to cook the lobsters for us for our supper.

Unfortunately this was the last time we saw Alfonso Rapu. We had found, with him as with other Pascuenses we talked to, that there was no strain in our conversation, no feeling of talking to someone of a strange and inferior race. We felt that his intelligence matched ours in every direction. Whatever the Pascuenses were they were not ignorant savages.